THE BIG BOOK OF
Jewelry Making
75 PROJECTS TO MAKE

THE BIG BOOK OF
Jewelry Making
75 PROJECTS TO MAKE

First published 2017 by
Guild of Master Craftsman Publications Ltd
Castle Place, 166 High Street, Lewes,
East Sussex BN7 1XU

ISBN 978 1 78494 1185

A catalogue record for this book is available from the British Library.

Publisher Jonathan Bailey
Production Manager Jim Bulley
Senior Project Editor Judith Chamberlain
Managing Art Editor Gilda Pacitti
Design Ginny Zeal
Photography Andrew Perris and Rebecca Mothersole

Set in Gibson and Rough Typewriter
Color origination by GMC Reprographics
Printed and bound in Malaysia

Measurements
While the conversions from metric to imperial are as accurate as possible, it is always best to
stick to one system or the other throughout a project.

Introduction

Creating your own jewelry is one of life's simple pleasures and it's great to feel that burst of pride when someone compliments you on a jewelry item and you know it is all your own work – and unique to you!

And the good news is – it doesn't need to involve complicated techniques and expensive tools. With just a few steps, this book shows you how to make simple, fun items in no time at all.

All the projects are really easy to customize or adapt to your own particular style. The designs also incorporate a range of techniques that you can learn to use such as wirework, beading, resin, and polymer clay.

This bumper book features 75 jewelry projects, from quirky to stylish, so there is plenty to choose from. Each project is accompanied by clear instructions explaining how to achieve perfect results, whether you are an experienced jewelry maker or just a beginner.

With such a dazzling array of earrings, bracelets, necklaces, and more, you're sure to find something to inspire you.

Contents

Kitty 294

Victoriana 298

Spirals 302

Zippy 306

Nala 310

The projects

millie

These cheery, colorful earrings bring a touch of spring. Tiny flower beads
clustered on chains are a simple way to make a lovely pair of earrings.
Made with lots of different colors, you'll find they match everything.

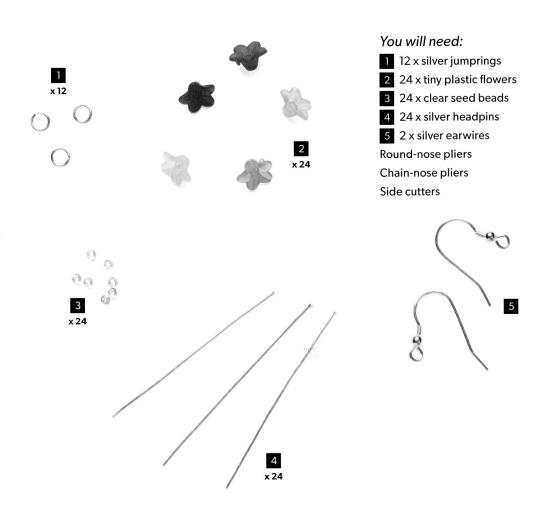

You will need:

1. 12 x silver jumprings
2. 24 x tiny plastic flowers
3. 24 x clear seed beads
4. 24 x silver headpins
5. 2 x silver earwires

Round-nose pliers

Chain-nose pliers

Side cutters

1 Take a headpin, a seed bead, and a flower bead. Thread the seed bead on the headpin first, followed by a flower bead.

2 Make a wrapped loop (see page 337). Make 24 flower pins in mixed colors.

3 Open a jumpring (see page 332), place two flower pins on it, and close the jumpring.

4 Take another jumpring, open it, place one flower pin, the jumpring with the flowers attached from the previous step, and another flower pin. Close the jumpring.

5 Following step 4, attach a row of six jumprings in total, with two flower pins attached to each jumpring. There should now be 12 flowers attached to the chain.

6 Before closing the sixth jumpring, add an earwire. Repeat this process to make the second earring using the remaining 12 flower pins.

Tip *To make this earring sit nicely you must have one flower pin in either side of the jumprings in the chain as you make it.*

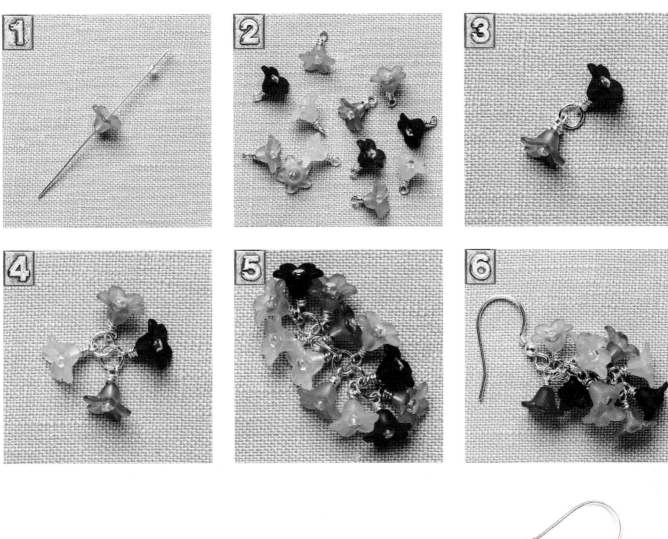

Tip *If you find making the wrapped loop a little tricky you can use the simple loop instead (see page 336).*

zoë

This silver charm bracelet is deceptively easy to put together. Use a variety of different colored beads to create a glittering rainbow. Make it today to wear tonight and heads will turn as you flash this little sparkler.

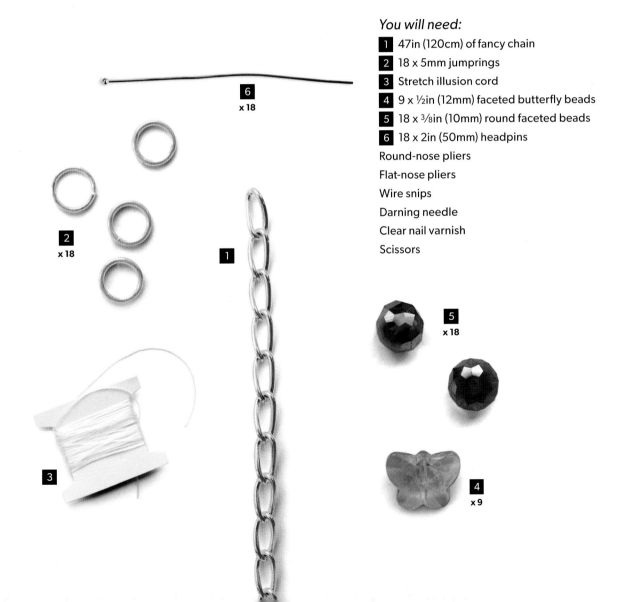

You will need:

1. 47in (120cm) of fancy chain
2. 18 x 5mm jumprings
3. Stretch illusion cord
4. 9 x ½in (12mm) faceted butterfly beads
5. 18 x ⅜in (10mm) round faceted beads
6. 18 x 2in (50mm) headpins

Round-nose pliers

Flat-nose pliers

Wire snips

Darning needle

Clear nail varnish

Scissors

1 Attach 18 jumprings at regular intervals to links in a chain around 47in (120cm) in length. The distance between each one does not have to be exact, but even spaces do look better.

2 Measure your wrist, then add on a further 12in (30cm). Cut four strands of stretch illusion cord to this length. Tie one end of the four strands to a link in the chain using an overhand knot (see page 347).

3 Thread all four strands through the eye of a darning needle.

4 Weave the needle in and out of every second link in the chain. This is not difficult, but it can be time-consuming, yet an even weave gives the best results.

5 To make the beaded charms, create simple eyepins (see page 334) at the end of each headpin just above the bead. Or you can wire wrap the pins to make them more secure. The butterfly beads here show a simple eye finished at the end of the headpins by using round-nose pliers.

To create the double-beaded charms, thread two beads onto a headpin, then make a wrapped loop (see page 337) or a simple eye at the end of the pin to secure them into place.

6 Attach the butterfly and beaded charms to the jumprings on the chain.

7 When you reach the end of the chain, undo the knot used to fasten the strands of cord and pull the elastic tight to fit your wrist. Keeping it tight, tie all eight strands together with an overhand slip knot, then cover the knot with nail varnish. Once it has dried, snip off the ends of the cord with scissors.

wildfire

The warm orange glow of this glass bead perfectly complements the bronze wire in this vintage-style wrapped-wire ring. For wire-wrapping techniques, a mandrel is essential to form the ring around.

You will need:

1 10in (25cm) length of US 16 gauge (SWG 18, 1.25mm) vintage bronze wire

2 12mm fire opal glass bead

3 Ring mandrel

Wire snips

Chain-nose pliers

1 Thread the bead into the center of the wire.

2 Hold the bead firmly against the mandrel and bend the ends of the wire around the back of the mandrel and return to the front. Don't cross the wires at the back.

3 Bend the long ends of the wire by hand to 90 degrees, one pointing up, one pointing down.

4 With your fingers, carefully shape the upward-pointing wire into a curve around the top of the bead and bend the lower wire into a curve around the lower edge of the bead. This creates an "eye" shape with the bead sitting in the center.

5 Twist the long end of the wire neatly around the shank a couple of times by hand. Repeat on the other side.

6 Trim the excess wire and squeeze the ends in with chain-nose pliers.

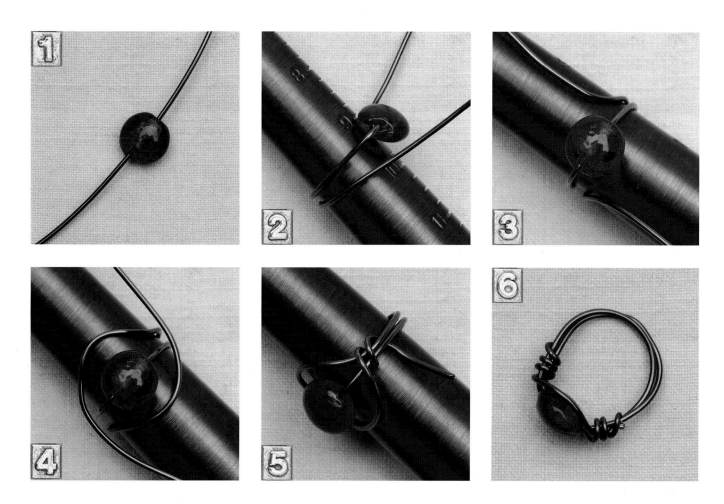

Tip *This ring works well with either a round or an oval bead. Ring the changes with different colored bead and wire combinations.*

emily

Cute as a button, this necklace is simple to make. The brightly colored flower buttons are stacked together to make a lovely summery piece. Pick lots of striking colors to add to the playful feel.

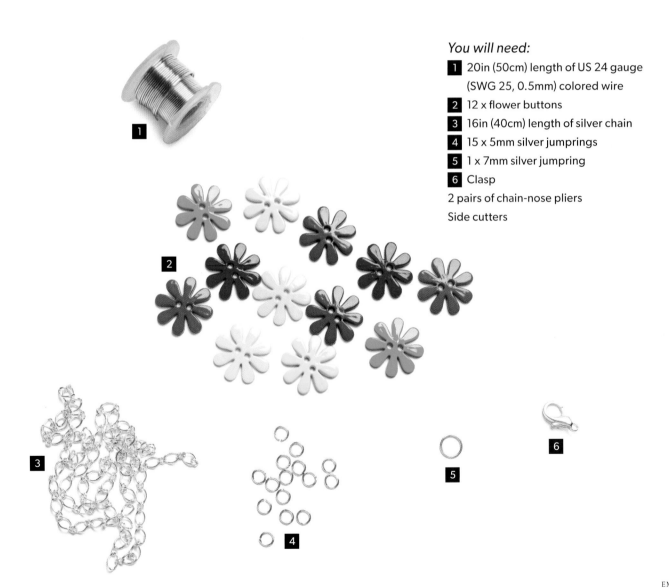

You will need:

1 20in (50cm) length of US 24 gauge (SWG 25, 0.5mm) colored wire

2 12 x flower buttons

3 16in (40cm) length of silver chain

4 15 x 5mm silver jumprings

5 1 x 7mm silver jumpring

6 Clasp

2 pairs of chain-nose pliers

Side cutters

1 Take the wire and thread on a button from the back through the front and to the back again. Place the button about 1½in (40mm) along the wire, twist the two wires together, and cut off any excess wire on the short side.

2 Add another button, coming through from the back again. Push that button until it sits just over the one already attached. Bring the wire through to the back, then add a third button in the same way.

3 Take the wire through all three buttons again, to tie them securely together. The picture shows them from the back; from the front you should just see two wires going through each buttonhole.

4 Attach three more buttons in a row above the two added in step 2. Thread all three on and take the wire under a couple of the wires on the row below. Go back through the top row of three again to secure.

5 To secure the wire end, wrap it around one of the wires at the back and cut off neatly.

6 Take the other six buttons and link a 5mm jumpring (see page 332) onto opposite sides of each one. Place to one side, leaving the jumprings open.

7 Split your chain into eight equal lengths. With a 5mm jumpring, attach one of the pieces of chain to the pendant.

8 Attach the other end of this chain to one of the open jumprings on a flower button. Close the ring. Attach the other chain to the other open ring on the same button. Repeat, attaching three buttons and four chain sections to each side of the pendant piece. Attach the final 5mm jumpring to one end of the chain and add the clasp before closing it. Attach the 7mm jumpring to the other end.

Tip *Wiring the pendant can be a little tricky so pay close attention to the step images. Use the main image to help you as well.*

señorita

Encase your hair with this adorable cage for a fresh, dressed-up look.
A lovely shiny bun makes the perfect background for this array
of pretty spring flowers.

You will need:

1 10in (25cm) length of US 20 gauge (SWG 21, 0.8mm) silver-plated wire

2 24in (61cm) length of US 23 gauge (SWG 24, 0.6mm) silver-plated wire

3 10–15 x fabric flowers

4 15 x beads (pearls and crystals)

Flat-nose pliers

Wire snips

Needle or nail file

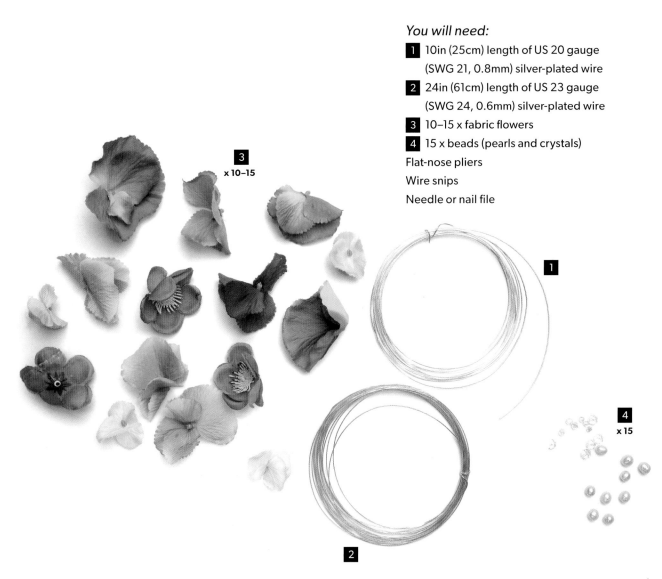

3
x 10–15

1

2

4
x 15

1 Gently bend the piece of US 20 gauge (SWG 21, 0.8mm) wire round into a circle roughly 4in (10cm) in diameter, depending on how much hair is to be covered. Holding the loop with your pliers, wrap each end of wire three times around the opposite end to close the circle up. Snip any excess wire off and press the ends in with your pliers.

2 In the same place, attach 18in (46cm) of US 23 gauge (SWG 24, 0.6mm) wire by wrapping it around the circle frame a couple of times.

3 Curve the wire with your thumb and forefinger, then thread on a bead until it's about 1in (2.5cm) from the circular frame. Hold the bead in place with a half-wrap (see page 338). Then smooth the wire into a nice curve again to continue.

4 If the flowers have a hole in the middle, thread the wire through that, add a bead and then pass the wire back through. If there is no central hole, make a hole in the plastic back with a needle so you can pass the wire through there.

5 Once you've added a flower to the wire, follow it with a bead secured with a half-wrap about 1in (2.5cm) along. Continue adding flowers and beads along the wire for about 6in (15cm). You need to curve the wirework to create a bowl-like shape that will sit prettily over your bun.

6 Tether the wire on the other side of the circular frame by wrapping it around firmly a couple of times. Then go back across the frame in a different direction adding flowers and beads as you go.

7 Keep going in this way until you're happy with how many flowers and beads are attached and the fullness of the design. You'll need to add extra pieces of wire by wrapping them around the frame, and doing single wraps around the wirework to give the whole design its structure.

8 Trim any bits of wire off with your snips, squeeze the wire ends in with the pliers and file any rough edges with the nail or needle file (see page 341). Try the hair-cage on and squeeze it into shape a bit. You might need to use hair grips to hold it in place, depending on how shiny your bun is!

Tip *You could add different lengths of chain to the wirework as you add the flowers. Loop them in or let them dangle a little.*

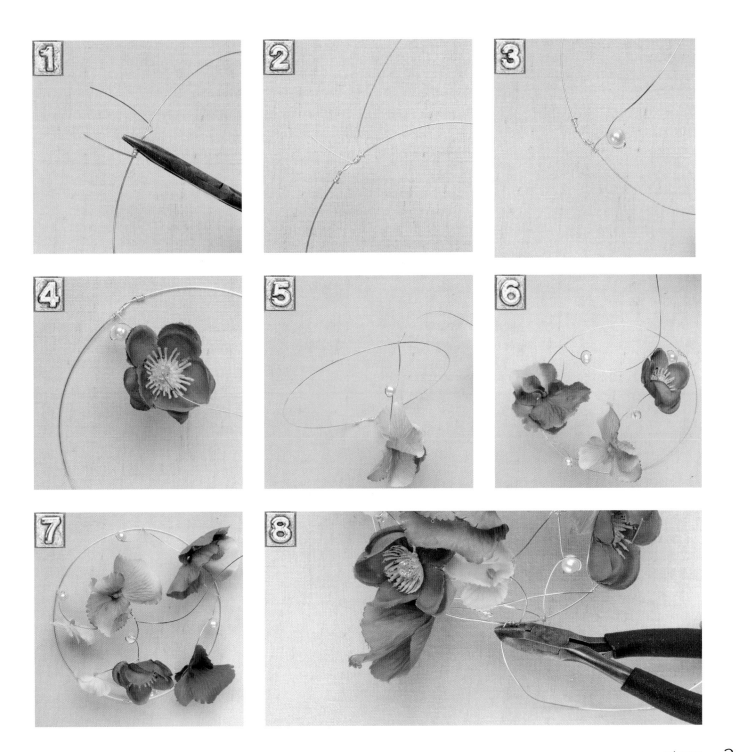

annie

This casting project is so deliciously simple you'll want to eat it. Just mix together some resin solution, pour it into a mold along with a pinch of cake sprinkles, and let the magic happen.

You will need:

1 Cake sprinkles
2 Heart-shaped rubber mold (approximately 8½ x 4½in (21.5 x 11.5cm)
3 1in (25mm) pin back
Clear epoxy resin
Disposable plastic cups
Stirring stick
Craft glue

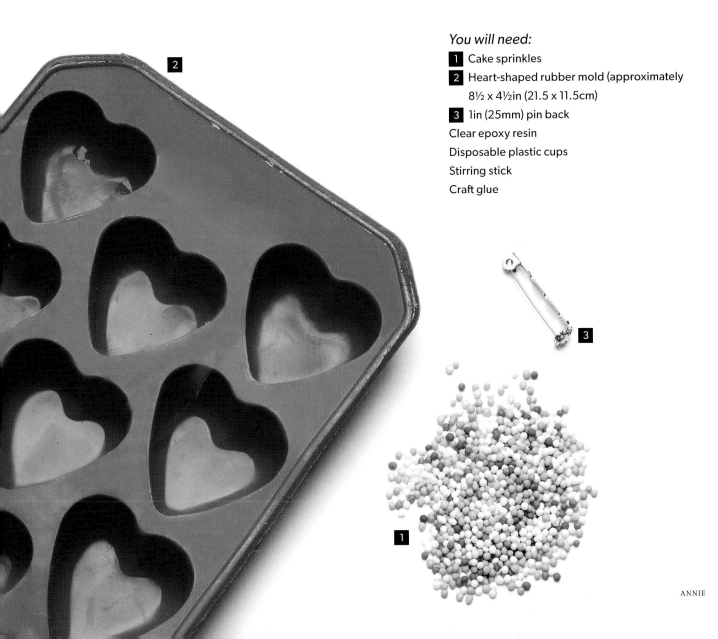

1 Line your mold with a light spray of cooking oil and mix together the clear epoxy-resin solution in a disposable plastic cup (see pages 352–53).

2 Pour a small amount of the resin solution into your mold, followed by a thimbleful of sprinkles, then more resin until the mold is half full. Cover and leave to set for 12–24 hours.

3 Turn your mold over and tap gently on the back.

4 Turn it over again and push the back firmly until your resin heart pops out.

5 Wipe off any remaining oil.

6 Turn your resin heart over and glue a pin back to the back.

Tip *If cake sprinkles don't get your mouth watering you can replace them with any tiny colorful morsels.*

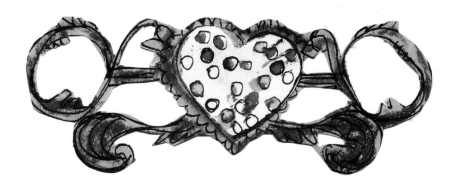

Tip *You'll know your resin has set when it is no longer sticky to touch.*

beady

Liven up your outfit by adding this striking chunky bead necklace. It is best to use fabric patterned with small details to show off the design on each bead.

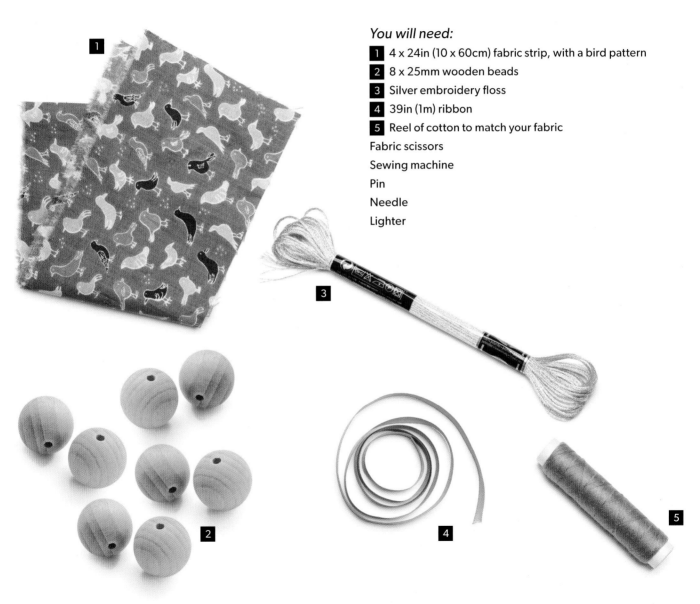

You will need:

1. 4 x 24in (10 x 60cm) fabric strip, with a bird pattern
2. 8 x 25mm wooden beads
3. Silver embroidery floss
4. 39in (1m) ribbon
5. Reel of cotton to match your fabric

Fabric scissors

Sewing machine

Pin

Needle

Lighter

Tip *Pull the material tight after putting the bead in the tube so the floss is wrapped close to the side of the bead and looks neat.*

1 To determine the width of your fabric strip, wrap it around one of the beads and then measure how much was used. Then add ⅝in (1.5cm) for the seam allowance and room to slide the beads in. Cut the strip.

2 Turn the strip over so the pattern is facing right side up and fold the strip in half lengthways. Machine stitch all the way along the open edge (opposite side to the fold), leaving just over a ¼in (5mm) seam allowance. Leave the two ends open.

3 Turn the tube of fabric inside out, so that the pattern is now showing. Fold the tube in half to find the middle and thread a pin into that point.

4 Slide a bead into the tube until it reaches the pin. Thread a needle with approximately 32in (81cm) of the embroidery floss, knot the end, and sew through the tube as close to the side of the bead as possible. Wrap the floss around the tube tightly several times, leaving enough to sew back through the tube and tie a knot. Trim the end neatly.

5 Remove the pin from the other side of the bead and repeat step 4.

6 Continue to add beads in the same way until you have six beads in the tube.

7 Slide in one more bead and make sure you have enough material to cover it and leave a hem allowance of ¼in (5mm). Cut off the excess material and fold the hem over.

8 Cut two pieces of ribbon to 17½in (45cm) and melt the ends slightly with a lighter to prevent fraying. Put one end in the tube with the bead and stitch to one side of the material with the teal thread.

9 Sew running stitch with thread all around the top of the tube and then pull on the cotton to gather the ends in together. Continue to stitch until the end is closed securely. Repeat steps 7 to 9 with the other end of the tube.

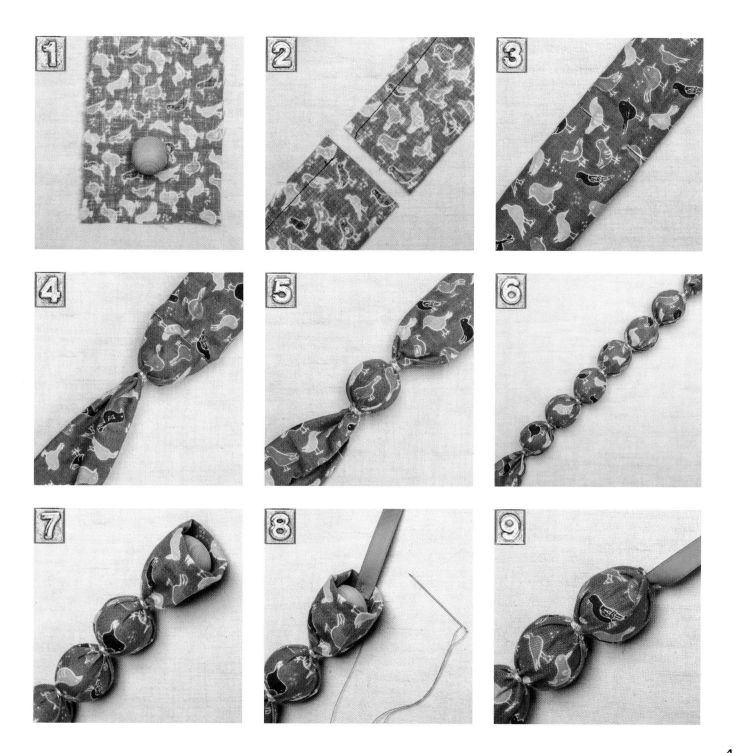

samba

Take your inspiration from a big cat and go wild with these leopard-print earrings! All you need to make your own beads is a permanent marker pen and a little patience.

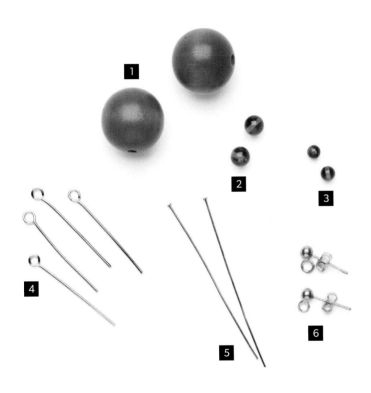

You will need:

1 2 x 18mm orange wooden beads
2 2 x 6mm amber beads
3 2 x 4mm amber beads
4 4 x 2in (50mm) gold-colored eyepins
5 2 x 2in (50mm) gold-colored headpins
6 2 x gold-colored ball post with loop earrings
7 Black and brown permanent marker pens
Round-nose pliers
Chain-nose pliers
Side cutters

Tip *Orange beads were used for the leopard-print pattern but any color would look great. Pick your favorite color to make your earrings unique.*

1 Take the black marker pen and a wooden bead; draw small, squiggly semicircles all over the bead with a small dot in the center of each circle. If you look at leopard spots, they are circular but don't make completely enclosed shapes. Be careful to keep the shapes even so that you end up with a regular pattern all the way around the bead.

2 Take the brown marker pen and draw in the middle of the circles, as shown.

3 Take an eyepin and thread on a 6mm amber bead. Make a simple loop at the open end (see page 336), then take a leopard-print bead and attach to an eyepin in the same way.

4 Take a headpin and thread on a 4mm amber bead. Make a simple loop at the open end.

5 Take one of the 6mm beads and open one loop; attach this to the leopard-print bead and close the loop.

6 Open the free loop on the leopard-print bead and add the 4mm bead on the headpin.

7 Open the free loop on the 6mm bead and attach to the loop on the earring piece. Repeat the steps to make a matching pair of earrings.

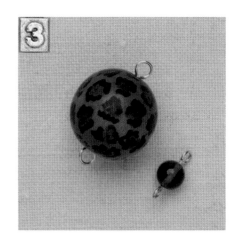

Tip *Practice the leopard-print pattern on paper before you start on the bead. The marker is permanent so you won't be able to correct it.*

cara

There is no need for catches with this adjustable cord bracelet. Striking glass European charms add a splash of color and pretty patterns to this straightforward bracelet design.

You will need:

1. 20in (50cm) length of colored waxed cord
2. 3 x European glass charms
3. Scissors

Tape measure

Tip *Make a few bracelets using brightly colored cords and different charms. Have fun layering them on your wrist!*

1 Measure your desired bracelet length around your wrist, then double it, and add half again. Cut that length of cord. String your charms onto the cord.

2 Loop the cord into a circle. Take the cord that is lying on top and make a fold 5in (12.5cm) from its end so the cord bends back onto itself (this is called the "working cord"). You should now have three cords side by side.

3 Loop the working cord around to the back, and underneath the other cords.

4 Wrap the working cord around the other cords again and take the end away from the bend, not toward it.

5 Make one more wrap around the cords as before.

6 Take the working cord's end and pass it back through the wrapping, exiting through the initial bend.

7 Hold onto the cords and pull the working cord's end to tighten the knot.

8 Turn the bracelet over and repeat steps 2 to 7 to make a second knot.

9 Trim the cord ends close to the knots. Slide the knots along the cord to open and close the bracelet.

Tip *Vary the design by threading on a charm holder and attaching dangling charms with jumprings.*

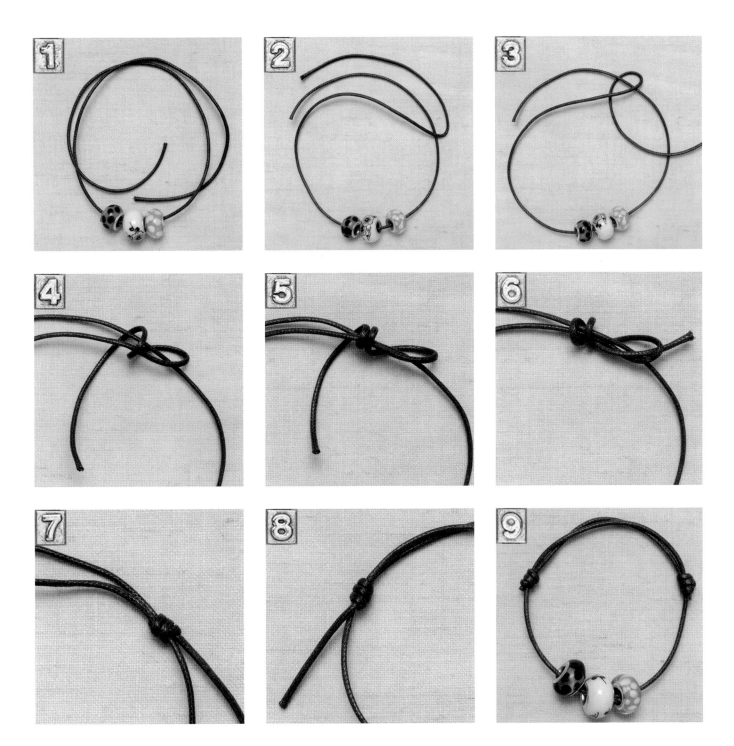

honeybee

Finding these wonderful bee charms provided the inspiration for this statement necklace of gold and black beads. With this technique it's all about the beads: using different shapes and colors to the ones shown here will create a dramatically different result.

You will need:

1 18in (45cm) length of black chain
2 3 x 4mm black jumprings
3 1 x ⅝in (16mm) large antique black bolt ring
4 50 x 2in (50mm) black headpins
5 50 x assorted shaped beads, 4–8mm in size
6 4 x 10mm honeybee charms
Side or top cutters
Round-nose pliers
Snipe-nose pliers

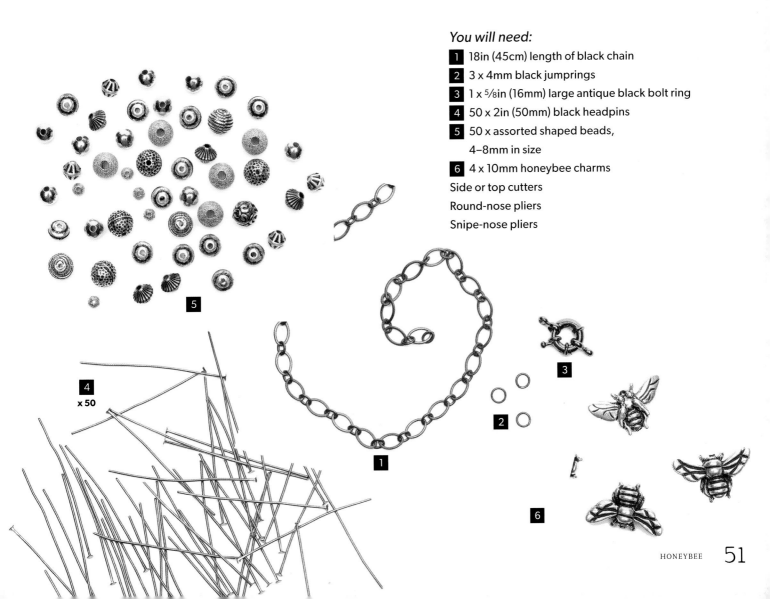

5

4
x 50

3

2

1

6

1 Cut 2in (5cm) off the black chain. Cut the remaining 16in (40cm) in half, so that you have two 8in (20cm) lengths. Add a 4mm jumpring to one end of one 8in (20cm) length of chain, link on the large antique black bolt ring and then close. Add a 4mm jumpring to one end of the other 8in (20cm) length of black chain, link on the other side of the antique black bolt ring and close.

2 Add a 4mm jumpring to the 2-in (5cm) length of chain, then link this to the other ends of both 8-in (20cm) lengths of chain and close, so that you have a necklace with a 2in (5cm) dangle of chain at the center front.

3 Now thread a headpin through a honeybee charm and, using round-nose pliers, make a hook as close to the top of the bee as possible.

4 Thread this hook through the very last link on the 2-in (5cm) dangle of chain and, holding the top of the hook with snipe-nose pliers, spiral the rest of the headpin around itself, securing the charm on the chain. Cut off any excess headpin.

5 Thread headpins through the largest beads, again making hooks as close to the tops of the beads as possible. If the hole of the bead is too large for your headpin, thread on a smaller bead first.

6 Thread the hooks at the tops of the beads made in step 5 randomly onto the chain and, as before, spiral the rest of the headpin around itself, securing all the beads onto the chain. Cut off any excess headpin.

7 Now repeat steps 5 and 6 with the remaining beads. There is no specific pattern, but it's nice to cluster the larger beads nearest the join of all the chains and use smaller beads as you work up the chain toward the clasp. As these beads are smaller, they will probably not require an extra bead to hold the eyepin.

8 Finally, following step 3, add the final three honeybee charms randomly to the chain so that they look as if they have just landed and are working busily away!

Tip *Think about using beads all either made from the same material or from the same color palette.*

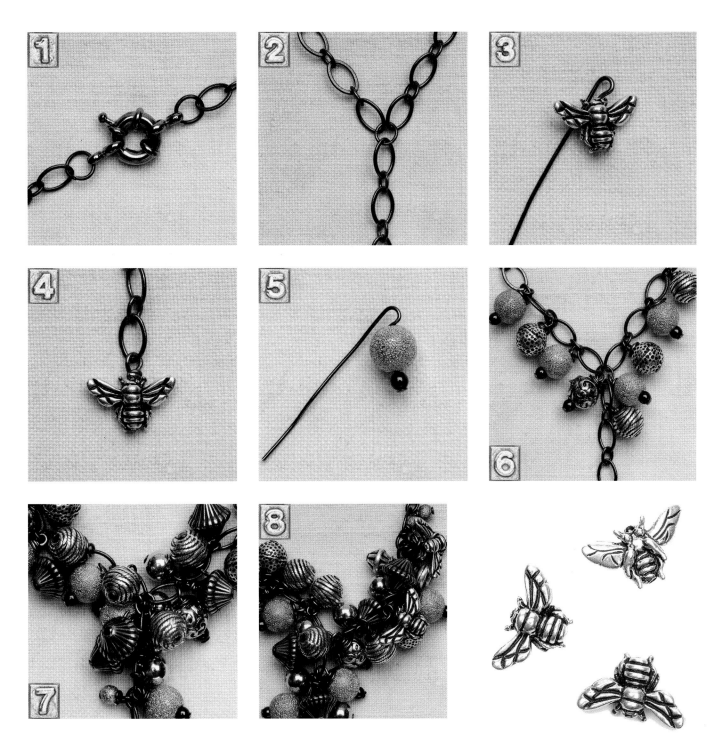

chichi

One of the rarest animals in the world but also one of the cutest, pandas take center stage on these striking earrings. With their bold black-and-white markings, pandas make an iconic motif for any design.

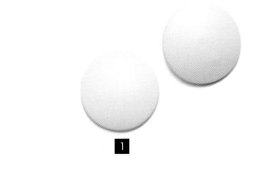

1

2

You will need:

1 2 x 15/16in (24mm) white, plastic self-cover buttons

2 Panda-print fabric

3 2 x 5/16in (8mm) flat-back earring studs with butterflies

Two part adhesive

Scissors

Craft knife

Needle

Green thread

3

1 Draw a circle approximately ⅜in (10mm) larger than your panda face on your printed fabric (see page 348).

2 Cut out the circle with a pair of scissors.

3 Using cotton and a dressmaking needle, sew a running thread loosely around the edge of the circle leaving the ends long.

4 Place the fabric over the white, plastic dome of the self-cover button and pull the two loose ends of cotton so it gathers tightly around the button. Check that you're happy with where the panda face is positioned and then tie the cotton ends together. Cut any excess thread.

5 Take the flat disc section of the self-cover button and snap it onto the back of the dome. It will click and lock into place. Use a sharp craft knife to cut away the excess peg from the back.

6 Mix a small quantity of two-part adhesive and glue the flat-back stud fitting onto the back of the button at the top. Repeat all the steps to make the other earring.

Tip *Self-cover buttons come in a variety of sizes so you can make large or small stud earrings.*

Tip *Double check the position of your flat-back stud fitting before gluing it to ensure your panda's face is the right way up.*

hannah

This gorgeous headband is a cut above the rest. Lovely beads are threaded onto wire to make the petals of this beautiful bloom. Perfect for any special event, this fantastic piece of jewelry is a real head-turner.

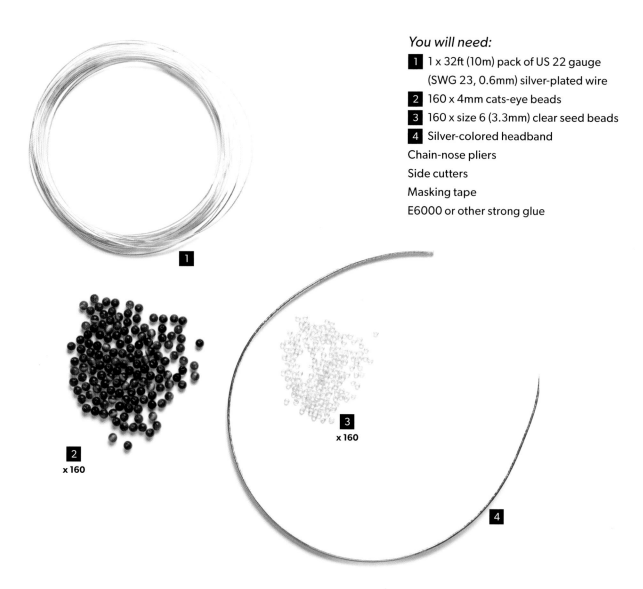

You will need:

1. 1 x 32ft (10m) pack of US 22 gauge (SWG 23, 0.6mm) silver-plated wire
2. 160 x 4mm cats-eye beads
3. 160 x size 6 (3.3mm) clear seed beads
4. Silver-colored headband

Chain-nose pliers

Side cutters

Masking tape

E6000 or other strong glue

x 160

x 160

1 Take the wire out of the pack and unwind the ends, holding the coil tightly. Let the coil release gently in your hand. The wire will settle into a natural coil about 4–5in (10–12.5cm) across. Cut ten single rounds from this coil and bend each one in half using chain-nose pliers to create the bend. The shape should look like a thin petal and the ends should cross over.

2 Take one bent piece of wire and starting with a 4mm bead thread on eight of them with a seed bead in between each one. Do the same on the other side of the petal, starting with a seed bead.

3 Push all the beads until the petal shape is tight, then twist the ends together. Twist for about ⅜in (1cm). Make ten petals in this way.

4 Take five petals and straighten the end wires on each one so they sit straight down from the petal. Gather the five together and wrap a small piece of masking tape around the twisted wire base. Wrap it as tightly as possible.

5 Add in the other five petals around the masking tape; make them as even around the outside as possible. Wrap another piece of masking tape around this, using just enough to secure them.

6 Divide all the wires below the masking tape in half and bend out to a right angle on opposite sides. Now bend the petals out one by one to make a double-layer flower with five petals in each layer.

7 Cut a piece of US 22 gauge (SWG 23, 0.6mm) wire about 12in (30cm) long. Take the headband and hold the flower against the band about one-third of the way up on one side. Lay the flower on the band with the wires running along the band and hold the flower and band together with one hand. Take the piece of wire and wrap around the wires and band, starting about ½in (12mm) from the flower stem. Wrap to the stem, bring the wire under the stem, and wrap for ½in (12mm) down the other side. Cut off any excess wire.

8 Cut off all of the wire ends at the end of the coils using the side cutters with the flush side against the wrapped end. Be careful of flying wires—try to hold the wires in one hand and use the cutters in the other hand.

9 To finish, wrap a section of wire around the stem of the flower to cover the masking tape. To make all the wire ends safe, use a cocktail stick and coat with a tiny amount of E6000 glue. Bend petals into shape.

Tip *This flower would look great made in crystals for a bridesmaid's tiara.*

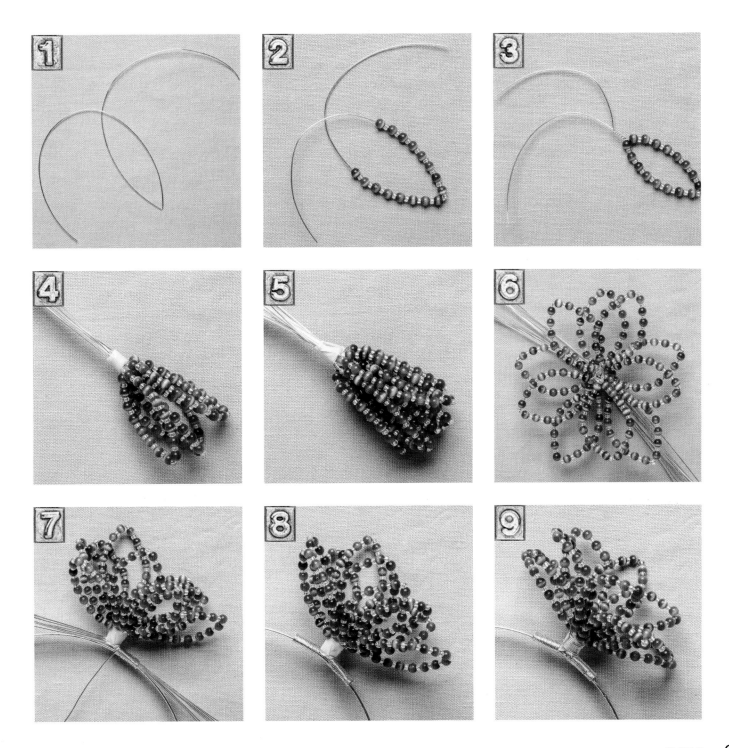

pebbles

Strand these glittering beads and colorful pebbles together to create a bracelet packed with glamour and style. A striking accessory for that little black dress, and for maximum impact, match your shoes and bag with it too.

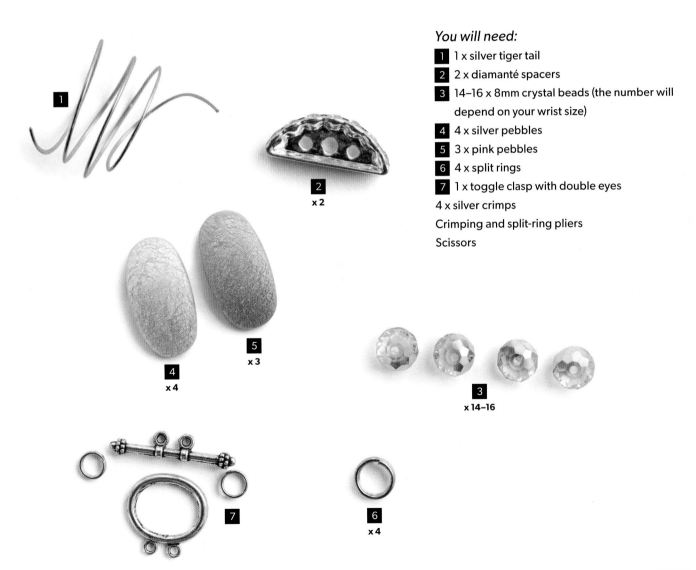

x 2

x 4

x 3

x 14–16

x 4

You will need:

1 1 x silver tiger tail

2 2 x diamanté spacers

3 14–16 x 8mm crystal beads (the number will depend on your wrist size)

4 4 x silver pebbles

5 3 x pink pebbles

6 4 x split rings

7 1 x toggle clasp with double eyes

4 x silver crimps

Crimping and split-ring pliers

Scissors

1 Cut two lengths of tiger tail to fit your wrist, adding a further 6in (15cm) to this measurement. Thread a crimp onto one end of each length. Make a small loop and then crimp the loops securely.

2 Thread one free end of the tiger tail through the top hole of the diamanté spacer. Pull the thread through until the crimp sits up against the hole.

3 Onto both threads of tiger tail, thread a faceted bead followed by a pebble. Continue this pattern until all the beads and pebbles have been used, then end with a crystal.

4 Thread the ends of the tiger tail through a second diamanté spacer and finish it off with crimped loops.

5 Attach split rings to the eyes on the toggle and the clasp, taking great care when separating the coils in the split ring (see page 335).

6 Finally, use the split ring pliers to reopen the split rings. Slide on the loops of tiger tail that are extending from the ends of the diamanté spacers.

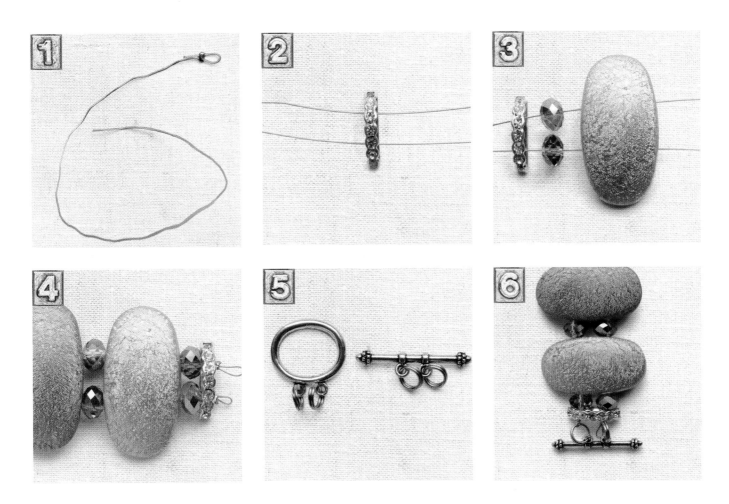

Tip *Faceted beads have both a mirrored and a faceted side to reflect the light.*
This gives an additional sparkle to the bracelet to make it extra special.

harmony

Inspired by the popular friendship bracelets, these rings are so simple you can make them for all your friends. We've used embroidery silks here but wool or any other brightly colored yarn would also work well.

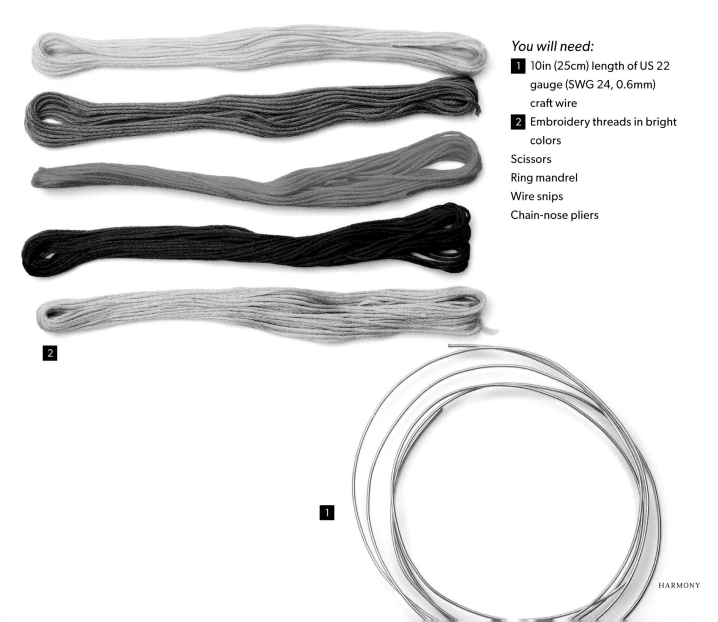

You will need:

1 10in (25cm) length of US 22 gauge (SWG 24, 0.6mm) craft wire

2 Embroidery threads in bright colors

Scissors

Ring mandrel

Wire snips

Chain-nose pliers

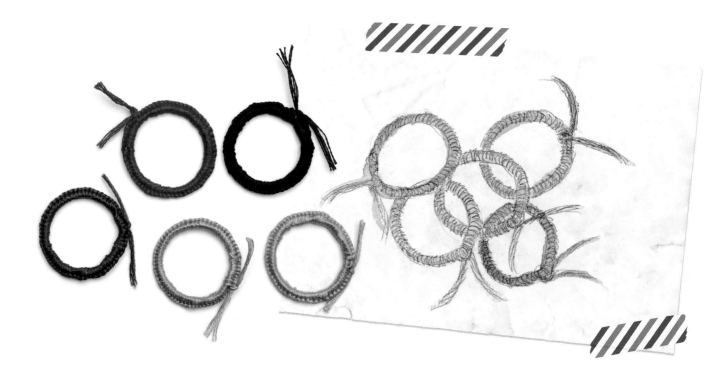

1 Cut 10in (25cm) of wire and wind the entire length around the mandrel at the correct size. Twist the ends together so that the circle doesn't spring open when removed from the mandrel.

2 Cut 39in (1m) of embroidery thread and knot the thread onto the wire ring. Leave a short tail of about 3in (7.5cm). Do not trim the short end—you'll need it later!

3 Work in an counterclockwise direction around the ring. Bring the long end of the thread up through the back of the ring and then push the end through the loop that has been created. Pull the new loop up snugly next to the original knot.

4 Continue making the loops, working in an counterclockwise direction around the ring.

5 When you have worked all around the ring, knot the thread onto the short "tail" left from the original knot in Step 2 and trim to approximately ⅜in (1cm).

6 Repeat Steps 1–5 with more lengths of wire and the remaining thread colors.

Tip *The ends of the wire should get hidden under the thread but if you can see them squeeze them in gently with a pair of pliers.*

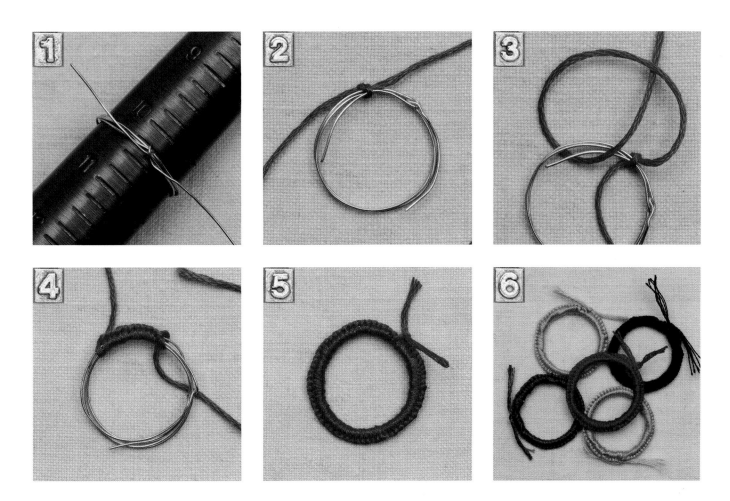

Tip *The trimmed ends of the thread will fray but don't worry, this is part of the charm of the friendship rings.*

writing

Send someone a subtle message with these simple and fun earrings. This technique is very adaptable and you can write whatever you want! Keep your wire on the roll-where possible cutting it off only at the last minute. You won't always know how much wire a word is going to take!

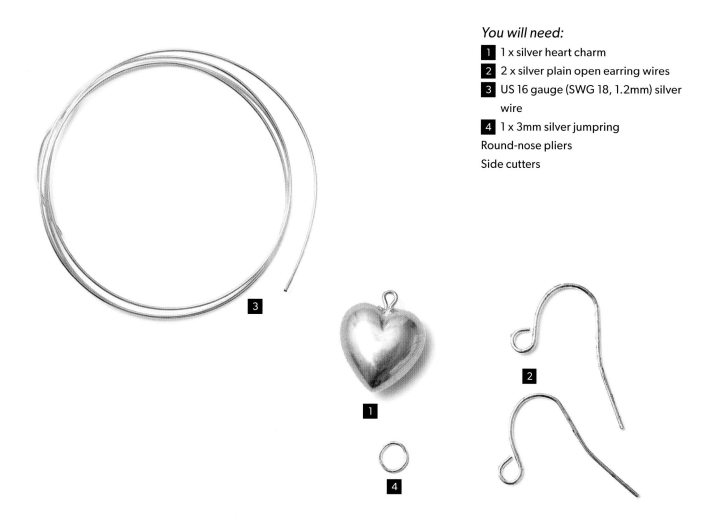

You will need:

1 1 x silver heart charm

2 2 x silver plain open earring wires

3 US 16 gauge (SWG 18, 1.2mm) silver wire

4 1 x 3mm silver jumpring

Round-nose pliers

Side cutters

1 Decide on the words you are going to use, then draw them to scale on a piece of paper to create a template.

2 Keeping the silver wire on the roll, use round-nose pliers to make a small loop at the very end of the wire.

3 Start your writing from this loop. You may find it easier to bend the wire with your fingers rather than use pliers all the time. Continue to follow your template with the wire until your word is finished.

4 If you wish to hang a charm off the end of your word, ensure you finish the last letter with a small loop and, using a 3mm jumpring, attach your charm.

5 Open the loop on an earring hook, then thread it onto the small loop of your word and close.

6 Finally, repeat the process to create the other earring.

Tip *The letters should all be joined up and their tops and tails evenly balanced so that the word hangs straight.*

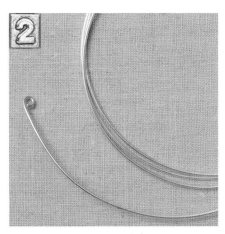

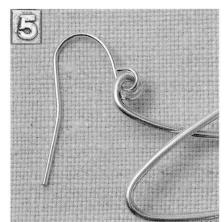

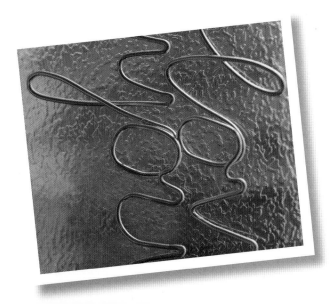

faerie

With this headband you'll be queen of the enchanted forest. This looks ethereal on crazy, curly hair. Lie down in the leaves and lichen wearing your crocheted faerie headband and let the daydreams begin.

You will need:

1. 36in (91cm) length of US 29 or 26 gauge (SWG 30 or 27, 0.3mm or 0.4mm) silver-plated wire
2. A couple of handfuls of moss, lichen or leaves
3. 20–25 x crystals or beads
4. 1 x tiara base

Large crochet hook

Flat-nose pliers

Wire snips

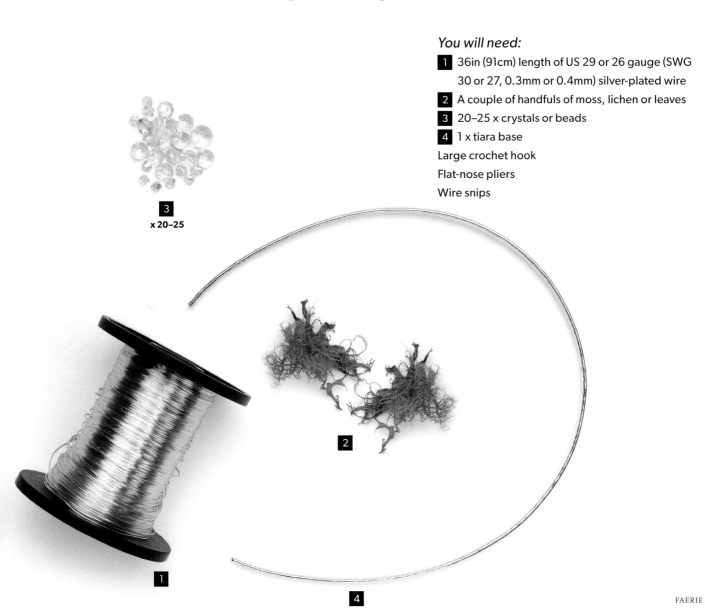

3
x 20–25

2

1

4

1 Cut a 12in (30cm) length of the wire. Make a loop in the end by just twisting the end around itself, then put your crochet hook through it from front to back.

2 Crochet a chain of loose loops about 8in (20cm) long (see page 342).

3 When you're ready to go back the other way and crochet into the first chain, hold the moss or lichen in small pieces behind the chain and crochet through it. Push the hook through the chain and then the lichen before you bring the wire around the hook. Continue to the other end.

4 You'll probably run out of wire by the time you get to the other end, so finish it off by pulling the wire through the last loop to tie a knot. Cut another 12in (30cm) length of wire and add it on by wrapping it through the last loop a couple of times.

5 Thread your beads onto the wire and make a little loop at the end of the wire so they don't all fall off.

6 Crochet into the second row of chain and lichen, adding beads as you go—just push each bead into place before you wrap the wire around the hook.

7 When you get to the other end, tie off the wire as before and snip off any excess wire. Then just shape your work a bit by pressing the beads to the front, maybe stretching out and flattening it a bit.

8 Wrap a 10in (25cm) length of wire 1½in (38mm) from the bottom of the tiara base (stretched into a horseshoe shape) and hold the crocheted piece across the base. Stitch through the crochet with the wire so it sits snugly across the base. When you get to the other end, wrap the wire around the base about five times to make it really firm. Snip off the excess wire, squeeze the ends flat with the pliers (see page 341) and you're done.

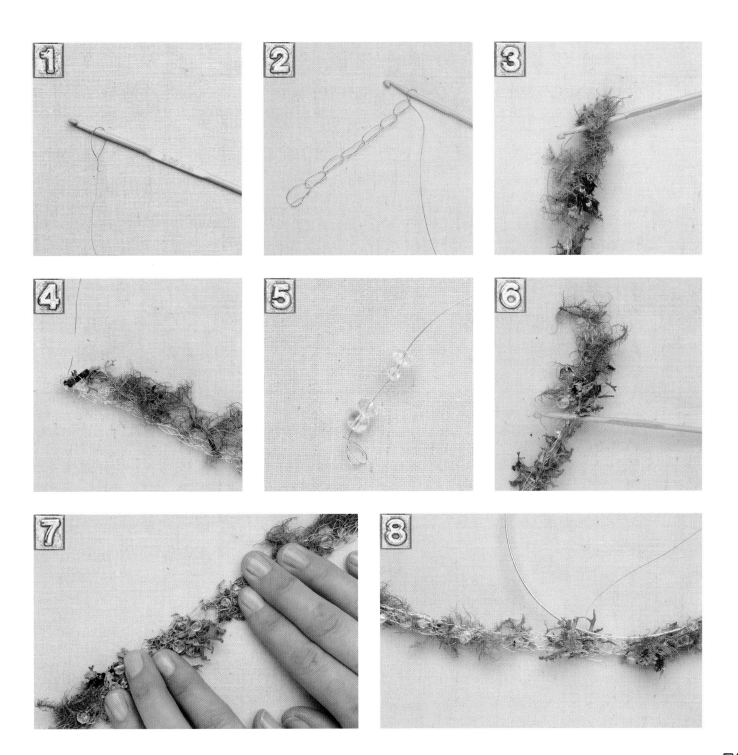

night owl

Metallic-effect, dark-colored clay gives these stylish cufflinks a masculine edge. There are numerous other colors available to try. Polymer clay is hard-wearing and lightweight, which makes it ideal for jewelry.

You will need:

1 2oz (56g) block of polymer clay
2 Owl head silicone mold
3 2 x cufflink blanks
4 Epoxy adhesive
Sticky tack
Aluminum foil
Baking sheet
Emery paper

1 Take half a strip of polymer clay and knead it on a work surface until it is really warm and soft.

2 Roll into a ball and flatten out into a disk shape. Measure it up to the mold and try to make the clay no bigger than the owl head. You may need to remove some of the clay at this point.

3 Keeping the mold flat, push and shape the clay into it, covering all of the owl head, including the ears. Try not to go too far outside of the owl detail with the clay and also keep the back as flat as possible.

4 Put the mold and clay into the freezer for 2 minutes to harden up. This will make it easier to remove from the mold without losing any detail. Carefully remove the clay from the mold and repeat steps 1–4 to make the second cufflink.

5 Place both clay heads onto a foil-lined baking sheet and put into a cold oven. Turn the oven on to 200°F (100°C) and bake the clay for about 15 minutes, then turn it up to 230°F (110°C) for another 15 minutes. Turn off the oven and let the pieces cool in there.

6 Sand the flat disk on the cufflink blanks slightly to create a rough surface for the glue to adhere to.

7 Mix some two-part epoxy adhesive (see page 351) and spread it evenly onto the flat disks. Put a small blob of adhesive in the center of the back of the owl head.

Tip *Silicone is ovenproof, so you don't need to remove your clay from the mold before baking it.*

8 Place the cufflink blanks onto the back of the owl heads and press and hold for a minute. Use a piece of sticky tack or polymer clay to support the cufflinks and keep them level. Leave for at least 14 hours before wearing, to be certain the epoxy adhesive is set.

Tip *Before you put polymer clay in the oven, cover it with a foil "tent." Take a piece of foil that will cover the clay, fold it in half, then open out slightly to form an upside-down "V" shape. Place over the clay so it does not touch it.*

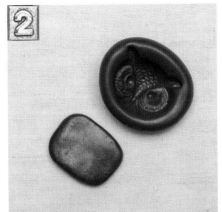

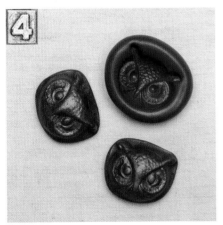

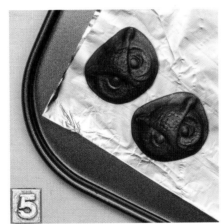

jacques

Give a lift to any outfit with this bright leather hot-air balloon. The movable basket gently swings with your every step, making you feel as though you could simply float away.

You will need:

1 Leather scraps in four colors
2 Strong thread
3 Small piece of balsa wood—
   4 x 4in (10 x 10cm)
4 Thin ribbon
5 Thin brass jewelry chain cut
   into 2 x ⅝in (15mm) lengths
6 1in (25mm) pin back
1 x patterned ribbon
2 x small brass jumprings
Clear nail varnish
Round-nose or flat-nose pliers
Scissors and craft glue
Needle suitable for leather

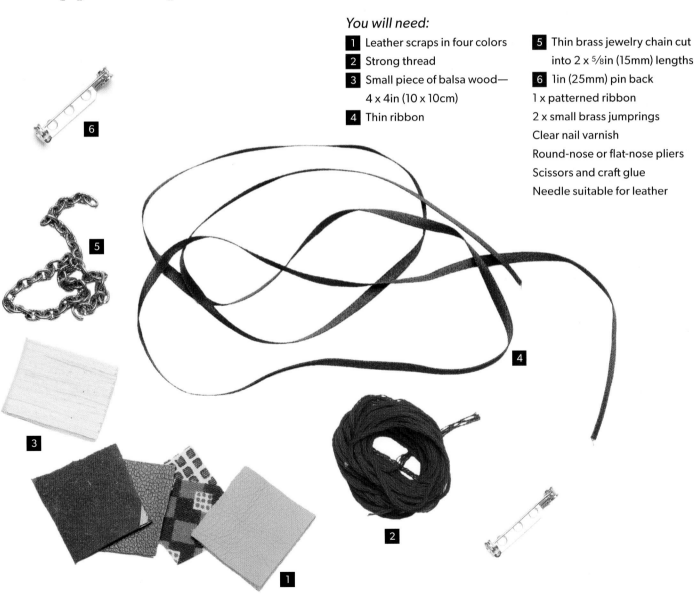

1 Cut out leather pieces using the balloon template.

2 Glue the smaller, decorative balloon elements into place on the larger balloon-shaped piece.

3 Sew from the triangle peaks of each piece to the peaks of the one below using a loose running stitch, finishing in a straight line at the base (see page 344). Don't worry if the back looks messy; you will be covering it up later.

4 Loop lengths of the thin ribbon around the bottom row of stitches and tie into a series of tight double knots. Trim so that only $\frac{3}{8}$in (10mm) hangs on either side of the stitch. Paint the ribbon ends with clear nail varnish to stop them fraying.

5 Use the template to cut out two "baskets" from balsa wood. Cover one side of each piece with glue and lay face down on the "wrong side" of patterned ribbon.

6 Leave the baskets to dry before trimming around the edges to remove excess ribbon. Glue the other sides of basket pieces and sandwich both $\frac{5}{8}$in (15mm) lengths of chain between them. Make sure the chains are parallel with $\frac{3}{16}$ in (5mm) exposed at the top.

7 Make two small holes at the base of the balloon $\frac{3}{16}$ in (5mm) apart. Use pliers to open the jumprings (see page 332) before looping them through. Thread the exposed ends of the chain through the jumprings and snap them closed with pliers.

8 Glue the final leather piece to the balloon back and secure the pin back.

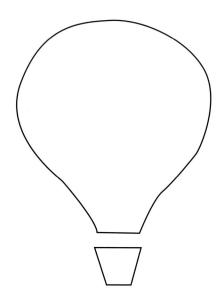

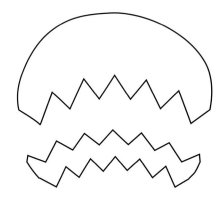

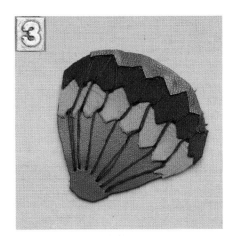

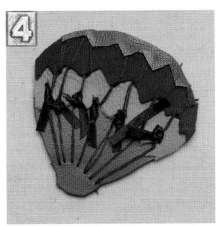

COCO

Be cool as a cat with this quirky silhouette pendant. Shrink plastic is easy and fun to work with, so any silhouette with a clear outline will work for this pendant but this stretching cat is an elegant choice.

You will need:

1 1 x 8 x 6in (20 x 15cm) sheet black shrink plastic

2 2 x 2in (50mm) black headpins

3 1 x wire choker with screw clasp attached

4 E6000 glue

Round-nose pliers

Small pointed-end scissors

White pencil

Pencil and paper

Craft heat gun (optional)

Photocopier

Tip *Shrink plastic comes in a variety of colors—this pendant would look great in any color.*

1 Photocopy the template below at 200 percent. Cut the paper shape out with the scissors.

2 Using a white pencil, trace around the shape on the matte side of the shrink plastic (see page 350).

3 Cut the shape out carefully using the pointed-end scissors. Shrink plastic can tear so be gentle when cutting out. When you get to the bit in between the tail and body, pierce through the center of the space with the scissors and cut out toward the line, then follow the line around.

4 Shrink the shape with a craft heat gun or in a toaster or electric oven at around 275–300°F (135–150°C); see page 350 and check the product instructions. For a complicated shape like this cat, the heat gun works better than an oven as you can control the shrinking more easily.

5 Take the black headpins and round-nose pliers. Hold the head end of the headpin in between the pliers about halfway along the jaws and wind around once to make a complete loop. Check the loop fits over the clasp on the wire choker before continuing. If it does not fit, then gently widen the loop by pushing it down the plier jaw a little more, then continue to coil the whole headpin. Coil toward the plier handles so the coil doesn't taper with the plier jaws. Make two.

6 Choose which side of the cat you want to be the front—one side is matte, the other shiny—and glue the coils on the back side in the middle of the cat's back, keeping the coils level. Leave to dry completely.

7 Unscrew the wire choker and thread the cat on to finish the necklace.

Tip *Solid shapes shrink better, so if you are struggling with the cat's legs and tail, try a different-shaped cat. There are lots of images available online.*

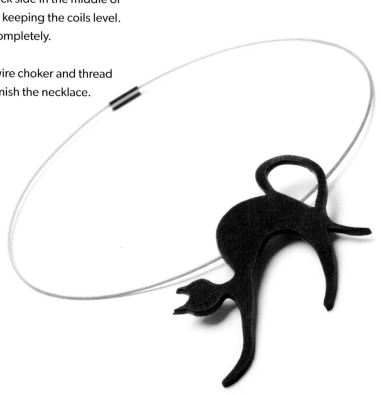

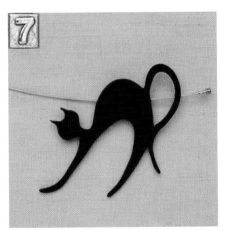

dreamcatcher

Inspired by the legend that a dreamcatcher lets only good dreams in, this bracelet is positively aspirational! This simple plaiting technique can be used with different materials to create either chunky or delicate, colorful or patterned designs.

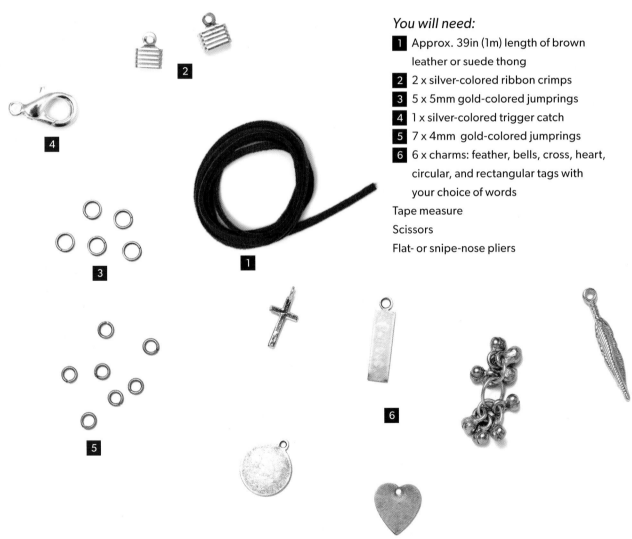

You will need:

1. Approx. 39in (1m) length of brown leather or suede thong
2. 2 x silver-colored ribbon crimps
3. 5 x 5mm gold-colored jumprings
4. 1 x silver-colored trigger catch
5. 7 x 4mm gold-colored jumprings
6. 6 x charms: feather, bells, cross, heart, circular, and rectangular tags with your choice of words

Tape measure

Scissors

Flat- or snipe-nose pliers

1 Wrap the leather once around your wrist, measure this length. Add on another third of the measurement again. For example, for a 6in (15cm) wrist length, add on another 2in (5cm) to equal 8in (20cm). As the bracelet will wrap around the wrist twice, double the final measurement to 16in (40cm) and add ¾in (2cm) to allow for the ends of the leather crossing over each other. The final measurement would be 16¾in (42.5cm).

2 Cut the leather to your calculated measurement and cut two more equal-length strips. Put the three level ends into the ribbon crimp.

3 Using the pliers, fold the sides over and squeeze tightly to secure the leather strips.

4 Plait the leather, trying to keep the widest part of the leather strip facing upwards so that the bracelet stays flat, not twisted.

5 Plait as far as you can to the end of the leather strips, then if necessary trim the ends so they are level. This is a good point to wrap the bracelet around your wrist to see if you are happy with the length. If not, trim it to the length you prefer. Place the level ends into the second ribbon crimp and secure as before.

6 Using the pliers, open the 5mm jumpring (see page 332) and thread it onto one ribbon crimp. Close the jumpring with the pliers. Open one of the 4mm jumprings and thread it onto the other ribbon crimp then thread the trigger catch onto it. Close the jumpring with the pliers.

7 Thread the six remaining 4mm jumprings onto each of the charms and leave open.

8 Thread each jumpring with a charm attached through one section of the plaited leather bracelet and close. Space the charms evenly around the bracelet, attaching some to the top section of the plait and some to the bottom section.

9 Fold the plait so that it forms a double bracelet.

Tip *Try three different-colored strips of suede plaited together or change the length of the strips to make a single or triple bracelet.*

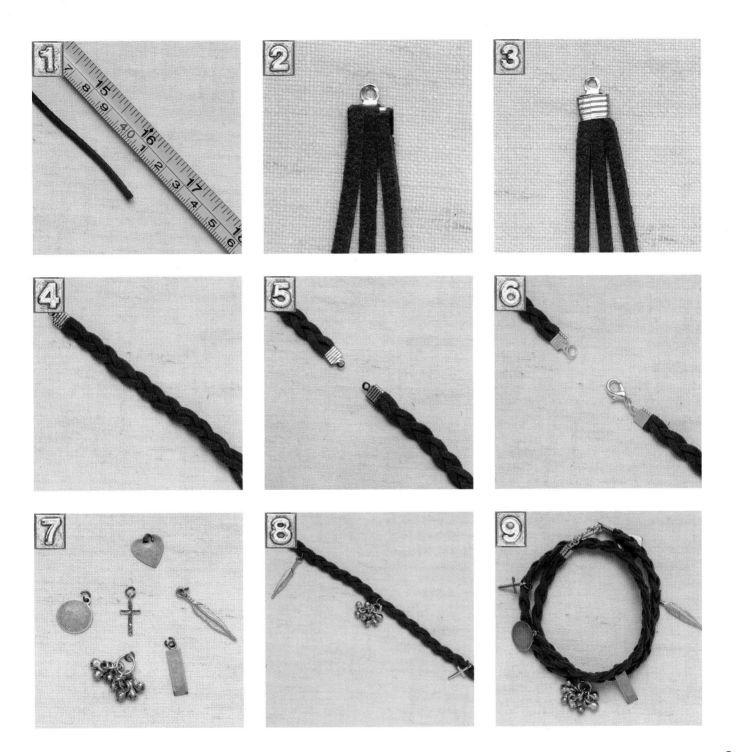

la mer

Attaching beads at intervals to a length of chain is a great way of obtaining a long necklace with a minimal amount of beads! Every day can feel like a summer's day when you're wearing this striking necklace.

You will need:

1. 9 x 2in (50mm) silver eyepins
2. 9 x 30mm large oval beads
3. 1 x 2in (50mm) silver headpin
4. 1 x 7 mm nugget-shaped pearl
5. 16in (40cm) silver trace chain
6. 1 x 20mm starfish charm
7. 1 x 15mm shell charm
8. 2 x 4mm silver jumprings
9. 1 x 7mm silver jumpring
10. 1 x 12mm lobster clasp

Side or top cutters
Round-nose pliers
Snipe-nose pliers

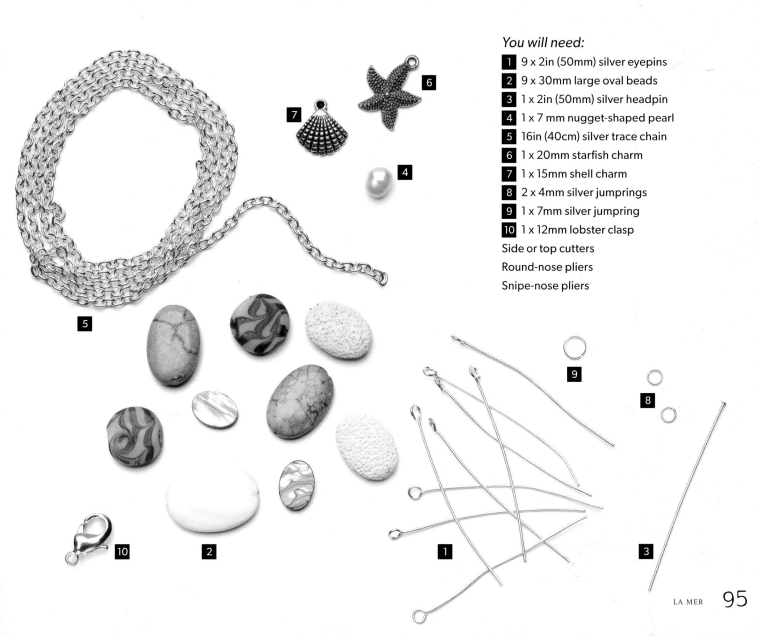

1 Thread a silver eyepin through a large pearl oval bead and make a large eye loop as close to the top of the bead as possible.

2 Now thread the silver headpin through the nugget-shaped pearl and make a hook as close to the top of the pearl as possible. Link this hook onto the smaller loop of the eyepin on the oval bead.

3 Holding the hook with snipe-nose pliers, spiral the rest of the headpin around itself on top of the pearl, securing it firmly in place.

4 Thread an eyepin through another large bead and again make an eye loop as close to the top of the bead as possible. Try to keep the eye loop sizes the same and do not close them just yet. Repeat for the remaining seven beads.

5 Cut 8 x 1¼in (3cm) lengths of chain from the silver trace chain, so that you are left with a 6-in (16cm) length. Cut this final piece in half, so that you also have 2 x 3in (8cm) lengths of chain. Starting at the large pearl oval bead completed in step 3, thread a 1¼in (3cm) length of chain onto the large eye loop made and then connect this piece of chain to the eye loop made on the next bead along, closing the loops as you go. Repeat this process until you have linked four beads on one side of the large pearl oval bead.

6 Starting again from the large pearl oval bead attach another 1¼in (3cm) length of chain to the large eye loop and then connect this piece of chain to the next bead along and keep repeating for the remaining four beads to make the other side of the necklace. Add one 3in (8cm) length of chain to the last bead on each side.

7 Re-open the large eye loop at the top of the large pearl oval bead now hanging at the center front of your necklace and link on the starfish charm and close the loop. You can also link on a shell charm to an eye loop higher up the necklace for that extra maritime feel!

8 Finally, add a 4mm jumpring to each end of the 3in (8cm) lengths of chain. Add a silver lobster clasp to one of the 4mm jumprings and the 7mm silver jumpring to the other one before closing.

Tip *Using gorgeous detailed beads can really give a strong theme to a necklace, as each bead has its own space around it.*

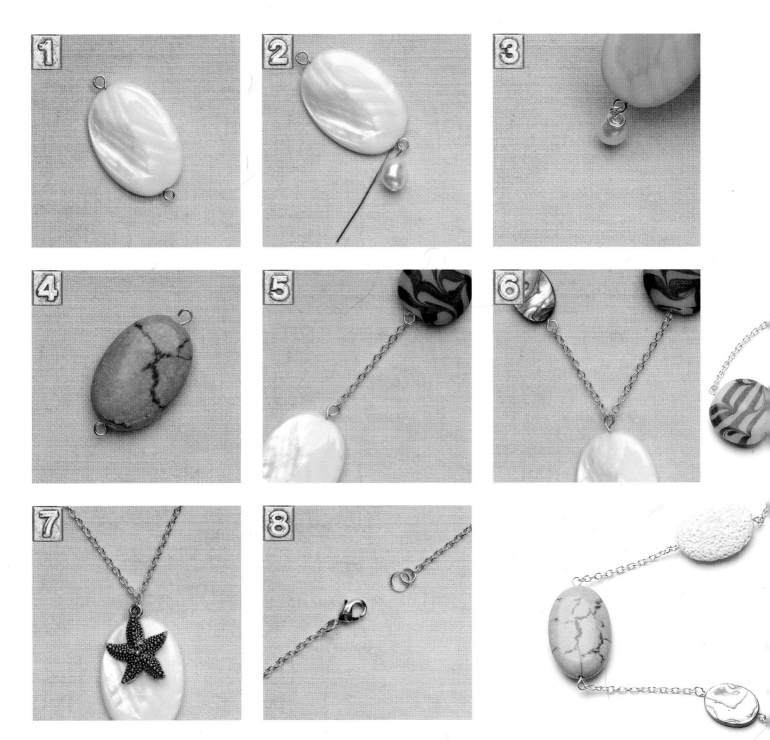

opo

The childlike quality of these enameled bottlenose-dolphin charms is matched perfectly with beach ball beads for them to play with. This fun kilt pin will become a firm favorite, just like the playful dolphins that inspired it.

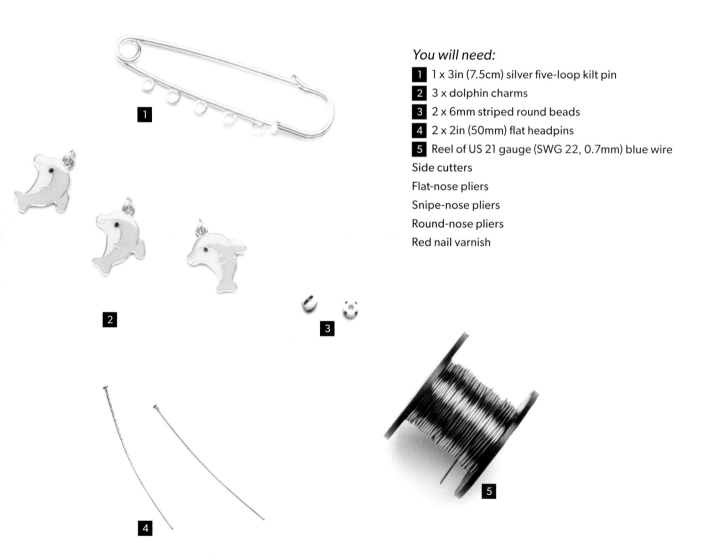

You will need:

1 1 x 3in (7.5cm) silver five-loop kilt pin
2 3 x dolphin charms
3 2 x 6mm striped round beads
4 2 x 2in (50mm) flat headpins
5 Reel of US 21 gauge (SWG 22, 0.7mm) blue wire
Side cutters
Flat-nose pliers
Snipe-nose pliers
Round-nose pliers
Red nail varnish

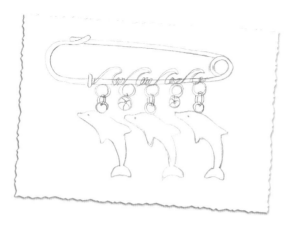

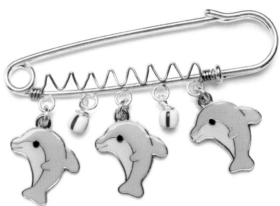

1 Cut 8in (20cm) of wire from the reel and bend it in half.

2 Slide a pair of flat-nose pliers right up to the fold and then bend the wire back over the jaw of the pliers, creating a zigzag shape as you work along the wire.

3 When you have made eight points, lightly squash each tip into a sharper point using your flat-nose pliers.

4 Stretch the wire out so it forms even points and fits on the kilt pin above the loops.

5 Coil the remaining wire tightly around the kilt pin either side of the end loops and then cut away any excess wire.

6 Open the jumpring at the top of one of your charms and link it through the first left-hand loop on your kilt pin and close. Repeat this step with the other two charms, linking one onto the middle loop and one on the end right loop.

7 Take your flat headpins and, using red nail varnish, paint the end of the pins and leave them to dry.

8 Thread a headpin through one of the stripy beads and form a hook as close to the top of the bead as possible. Thread this hook through the second empty loop along on the kilt pin.

9 Grip the hook in the jaws of your snipe-nose pliers. Wrap the long end of wire on the headpin around the base of the hook, forming a spiral of wire on top of the bead. Cut away any excess wire. Attach the other stripy bead to the remaining empty loop on the kilt pin in the same way.

Tip *When painting nail varnish onto a headpin it is best to lightly sand the head of the pin with a piece of emery paper first so the color adheres to the metal.*

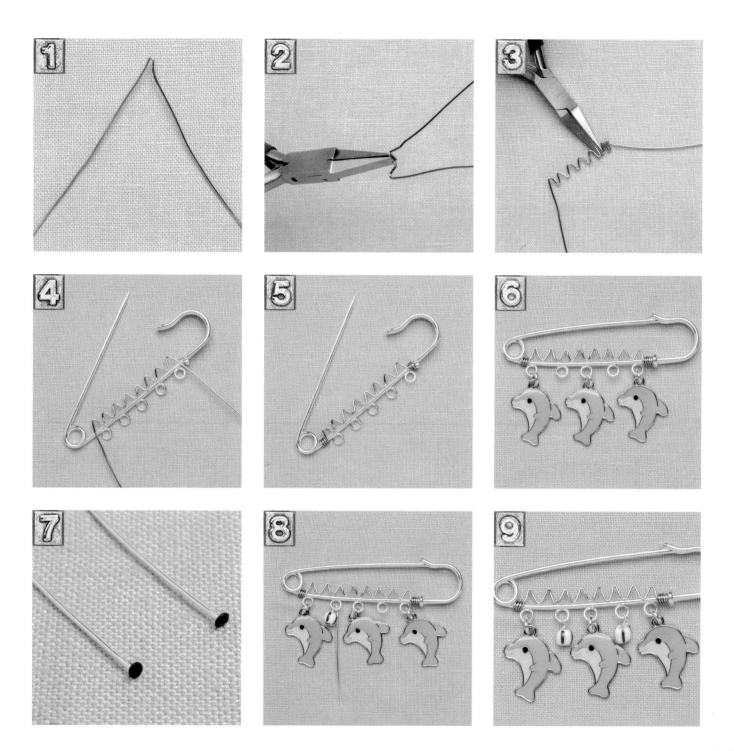

alice

These cute paper and resin earrings will add charm to any outfit. Using pretty floral paper and a little resin, these are so quick and easy to make, you can make a pair to match every mood.

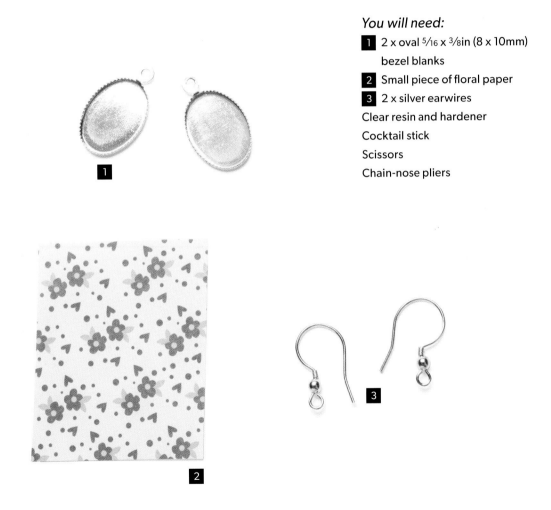

You will need:

1 2 x oval ⁵⁄₁₆ x ³⁄₈in (8 x 10mm) bezel blanks

2 Small piece of floral paper

3 2 x silver earwires

Clear resin and hardener

Cocktail stick

Scissors

Chain-nose pliers

Tip *When mixing the resin, stir very gently to avoid creating bubbles.*

1 On the flower paper, draw around the pendant twice with a pencil.

2 Then cut out the two shapes about ¹⁄₃₂in (1mm) inside the pencil line.

3 Cut out a few extra flowers.

4 Make up the clear resin to the manufacturer's instructions and lay the papers in the bottom of the blanks.

5 Add a layer of resin in each blank and then gently place in the extra flowers. Use a cocktail stick to move the flowers into the right position.

6 Leave the resin to dry completely. Attach the blanks to earwires to finish.

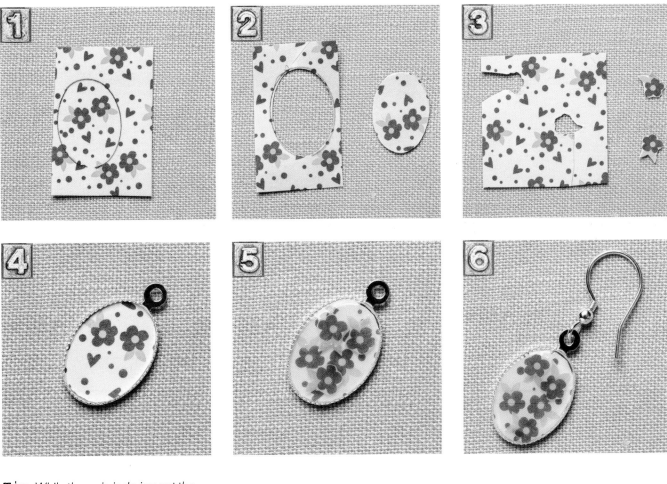

Tip *While the resin is drying put the earrings under a cup to stop dust getting stuck to the surface.*

mille

Millefiori is a combination of two Italian words, "mille" (thousand) and "fiori" (flowers). With their bright and vibrant colors, these millefiori beads are perfect for this bright, emotive bracelet!

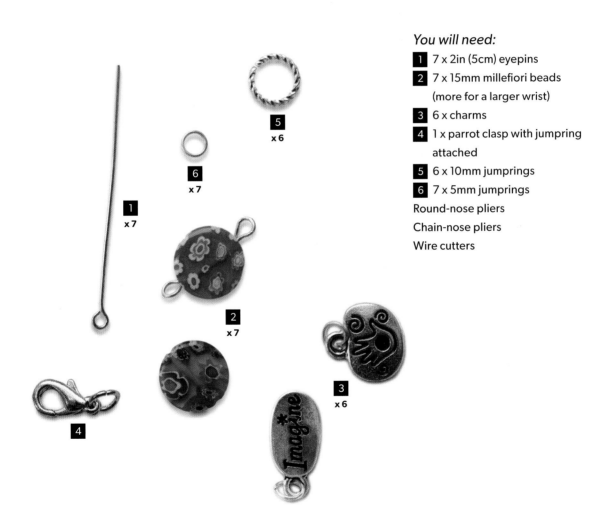

You will need:

1. 7 x 2in (5cm) eyepins
2. 7 x 15mm millefiori beads (more for a larger wrist)
3. 6 x charms
4. 1 x parrot clasp with jumpring attached
5. 6 x 10mm jumprings
6. 7 x 5mm jumprings

Round-nose pliers

Chain-nose pliers

Wire cutters

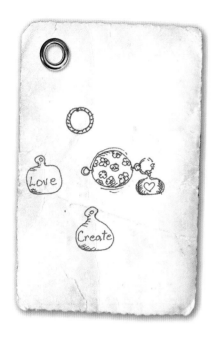

1 Select the millefiori beads you wish to use in your bracelet.

2 Thread an eyepin through each bead. Make a 90-degree bend on the eyeless piece of wire that juts out.

3 Snip off all but ¼in (6mm) of the wire eyepin. Grip the end of the pin in round-nose pliers to make another eye in the wire (see page 334).

4 Attach 5mm jumprings to each of the charms, then close them. Those used in the illustrated bracelet are double-sided with a symbol that matches the text.

5 Open all the 10mm jumprings. Link a millefiori bead to each one, then link a charm, followed by another linked bead. Close all the jumprings securely.

6 Continue to link all the beads and charms together in a chain. Finish the bracelet off with a millefiori bead.

7 Using the small jumpring that is already attached to the parrot clasp, fasten the clasp to an eye on the end of one of the last millefiori beads. Finish off by attaching a jumpring to the remaining eye and clipping the whole bracelet closed.

cocktail

This stunning ring introduces the skill of weaving beads onto a wire frame. The technique requires a little more patience than some of the others in this book but the results are quite spectacular.

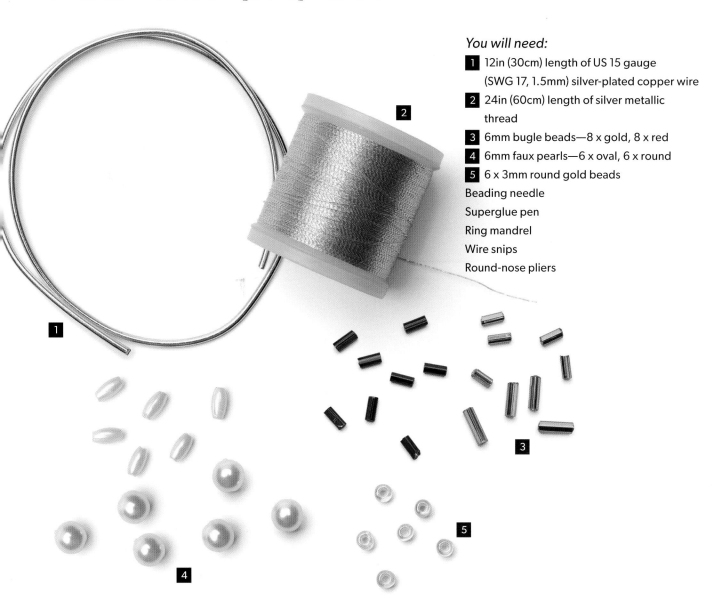

You will need:

1. 12in (30cm) length of US 15 gauge (SWG 17, 1.5mm) silver-plated copper wire
2. 24in (60cm) length of silver metallic thread
3. 6mm bugle beads—8 x gold, 8 x red
4. 6mm faux pearls—6 x oval, 6 x round
5. 6 x 3mm round gold beads

Beading needle
Superglue pen
Ring mandrel
Wire snips
Round-nose pliers

1 Cut 12in (30cm) of wire and make a small loop at one end with round-nose pliers.

2 Hold the loop flat against the mandrel and wrap the wire twice around the mandrel. Trim the end of the wire leaving approximately ⅜in (1cm) extra.

3 Use round-nose pliers to make the second loop, which completes the wire frame. Put the ring back onto the mandrel and adjust if necessary to make a pleasing shape.

4 Cut 24in (60cm) of metallic thread and knot it onto the frame, close to one of the end loops. Dot the knot with superglue to hold it in place. Allow the glue to dry completely then trim the short end close to the knot.

5 Thread the other end of the metallic thread onto the beading needle. Begin with one of the gold bugle beads, pull it up close to the knot then weave the thread around the frame, behind the gold bead then back to the starting point.

6 Repeat with the remaining gold bugle beads until this row is filled. Dot the thread with glue at the end of the row to hold the beads in place.

7 Begin the second row by weaving the oval faux pearls between the wire frame in the same way. Continue to fill this row with the pearls and small gold beads.

8 At the end of the second row, dot the thread with glue to hold the beads in place, then turn to the final row and weave the red bugle beads into place. Knot the thread onto the frame, dot it with glue and neatly trim the end.

9 Apply a little glue to the end loops and add the round faux pearls. Once the design is finished, dot some glue over the thread on the back of the frame so it will secure all the beads but not be visible.

Tip *A superglue pen is invaluable for this project as it delivers a very small amount of glue to exactly the right spot.*

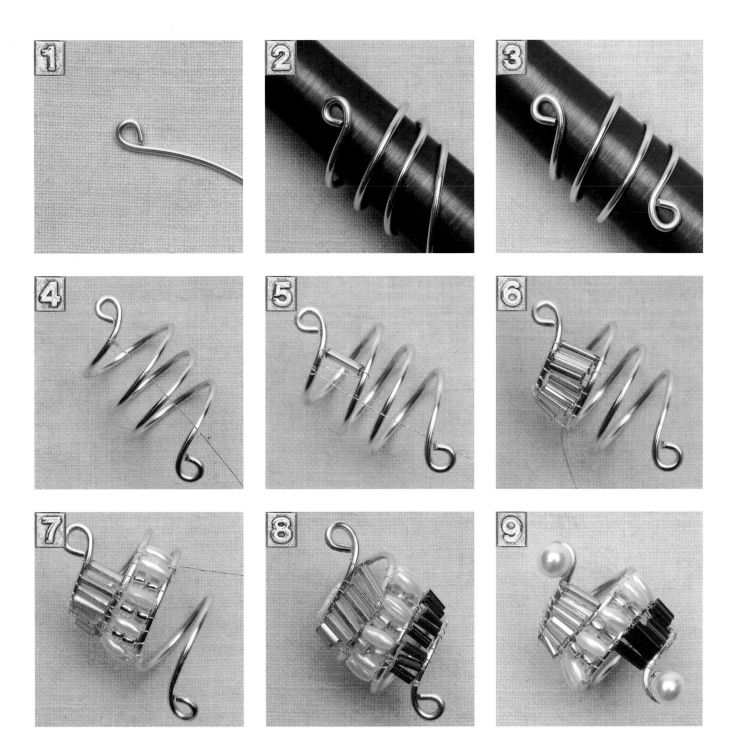

shapes

This classic heart design looks stunning and the main element is made from only one single length of wire. It looks equally as attractive left simple or with an additional bead for a splash of color and sparkle.

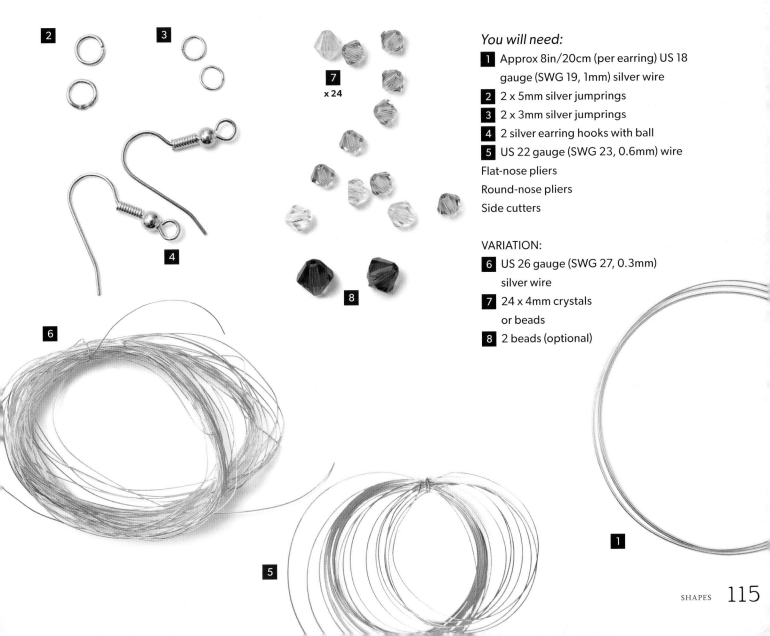

x 24

You will need:

1 Approx 8in/20cm (per earring) US 18 gauge (SWG 19, 1mm) silver wire

2 2 x 5mm silver jumprings

3 2 x 3mm silver jumprings

4 2 silver earring hooks with ball

5 US 22 gauge (SWG 23, 0.6mm) wire

Flat-nose pliers

Round-nose pliers

Side cutters

VARIATION:

6 US 26 gauge (SWG 27, 0.3mm) silver wire

7 24 x 4mm crystals or beads

8 2 beads (optional)

1 Cut off 8in (20cm) of US 18 gauge (SWG 19, 1mm) wire. Form a loose loop roughly in the center of the wire. For the variation, add a bead to settle in the middle of this loop.

2 Holding both ends of the wire, bend them round symmetrically to form a heart shape.

3 Using flat-nose pliers, make one end of the wire straight where the two wires cross at the bottom of the heart.

4 Spiral the other end of the wire around the straight end of the wire a couple of times. Cut away any excess using side cutters.

5 With the remaining length of straight wire, form an eye loop and again cut away any excess wire.

6 Open a 5mm jumpring and link this to the top of the heart and to a 3mm jumpring, then close.

7 Open the loop on an earring wire, link the 3mm jumpring to it and close.

8 Make wire balls by scrunching a length of wire and continue to keep wrapping the wire around itself until it is approximately ⅜in (10mm) in diameter. Leave a length of wire long enough to make an eye loop at the top of your wire ball bead. Attach the wire ball to the loop at the bottom of the heart.

9 Finally, repeat the process to create the other earring. For the variation, you can make your own beaded balls by threading beads on to a length of wire and tying them together.

Tip *When making beaded balls, be sure to leave a piece of wire or nylon at one end that is long enough to turn into an eye loop.*

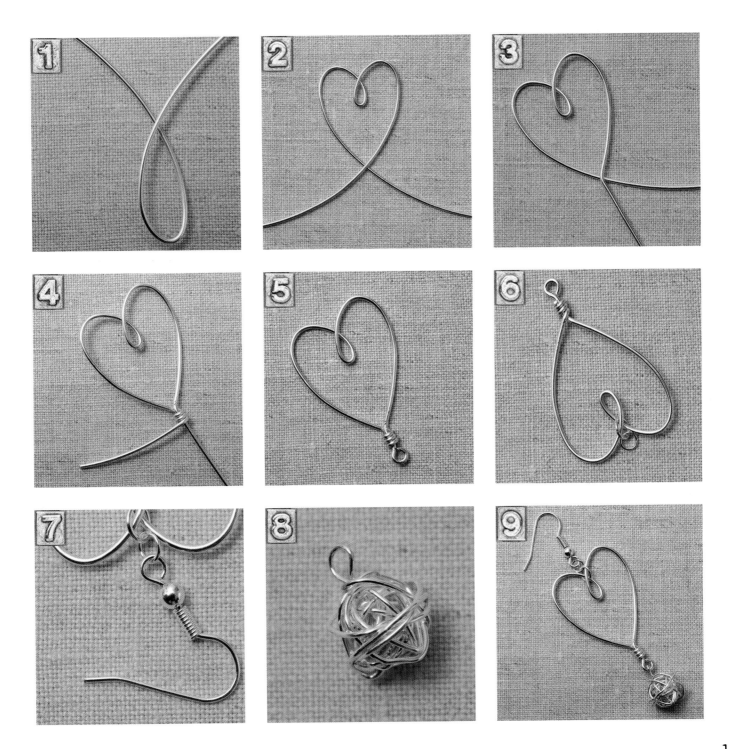

clarice

A vintage-style comb is a lovely way to give your hair a subtle bit of vintage glamour. Combine an old brooch with fabric foliage for an elegant decoration. Or make two to embellish a 1940s-style victory roll.

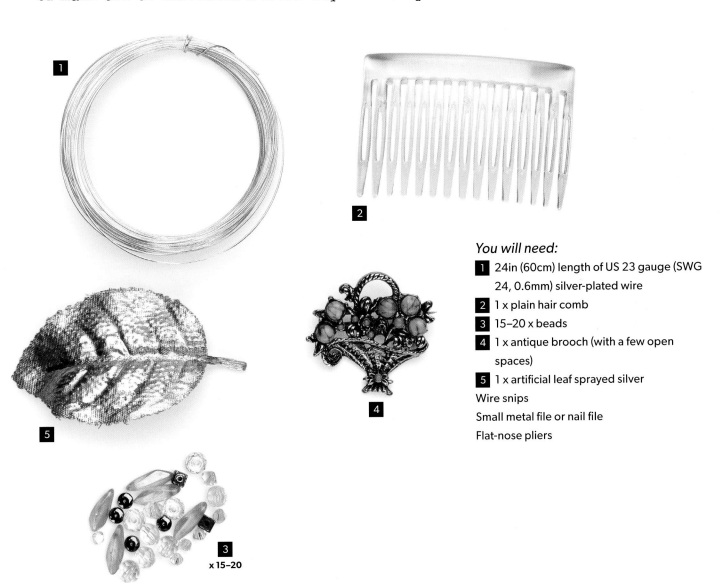

You will need:

1. 24in (60cm) length of US 23 gauge (SWG 24, 0.6mm) silver-plated wire
2. 1 x plain hair comb
3. 15–20 x beads
4. 1 x antique brooch (with a few open spaces)
5. 1 x artificial leaf sprayed silver

Wire snips

Small metal file or nail file

Flat-nose pliers

x 15–20

1 Wrap one end of the piece of wire around the top of the comb between the last two prongs about three times.

2 Choose your first bead and thread it onto the free end of the wire. Move it down the wire until it is about ½in (1cm) from the comb and then wrap the wire around the bead, from one hole to the other, to hold the bead in place (see page 338).

3 Using your thumb and forefinger, smooth the wire into a curve and then add your next bead. Wrap the wire around it again from one hole to the other to hold it in place, then wrap the wire once around the comb a couple of prongs along to make your desired curved shape.

4 Work your way along the top of the comb in this way, adding more beads and attaching the wire to the top of the comb a couple of times. Then work your way back to where you started in the same way. To make the decoration look less uniform, try occasionally curving the wire upward instead of down before you attach the next bead, so that it sits on the other side of the wire.

Tip *Instead of beads try using sparkly vintage crystals or cut-up pieces of diamanté or semiprecious stones.*

5 Prepare your brooch by snipping the pin off the back. Using your snips, cut through the pin close to the hinge in a careful, controlled way so the pin doesn't fly off. Gently snip the pin base in one direction, then the other. If it's a bit tough, just take your time and keep snipping round in different directions. File the sharp edge left behind to make it smooth.

6 Attach the brooch to the end of your comb simply by finding a hole in the brooch structure, threading the wire through and wrapping it around the comb (in two places ideally).

7 Attach the artificial leaf behind the brooch by pushing the wire gently through the leaf or stalk and moving it down into place.

Tip *When you remove the back of the brooch, try not to pull it back and forth too much as you can end up loosening stones.*

8 Carry on adding beads to your design in a similar way as before. To build the design upward, away from the comb, wrap the wire around the initial wirework instead of the comb.

9 When you get to the other end of the comb, wrap the remaining wire around the last prong three times to secure it, squeezing it with your pliers to make sure it's nice and tight (see page 341). Snip any excess wire off, then style your hair and try it on!

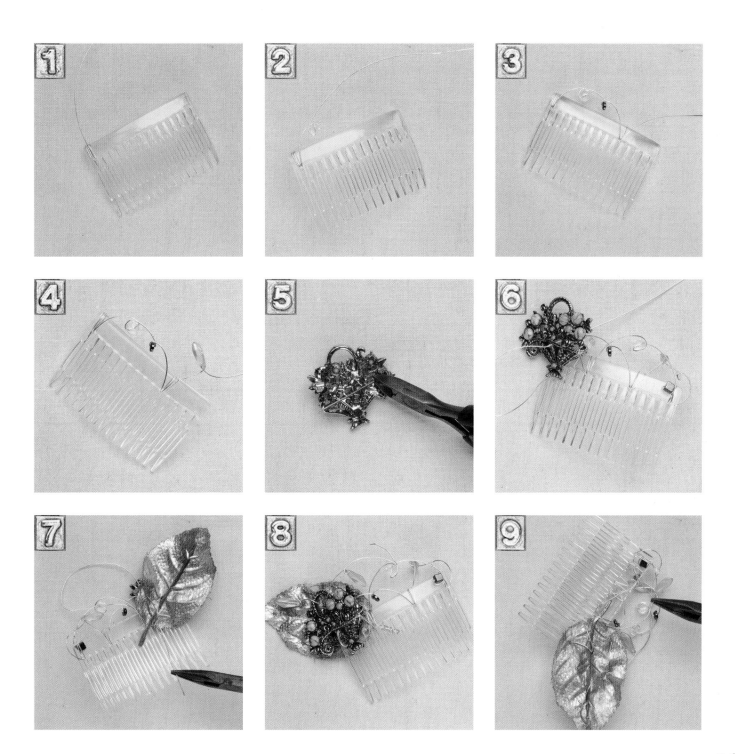

decoupage

Decoupage (decorating a surface with paper cutouts) is a great way to incorporate illustrations into your designs. This is the perfect project to revamp your old bangles, but you can also buy blank bangles in wood or plastic in any size or style you desire.

You will need:

1 3 x different sheets of standard size wrapping paper with bird motifs

2 White (PVA) glue

3 1 x bangle

4 Clear varnish

Scissors

Tape measure

Glue brush

Tip *Pour the glue into a pot and cover the surface you are working on as this can get messy!*

1 Cut out 1¼in (3cm) squares, and smaller, of bird images from different wrapping papers. Also cut some thinner strips and rectangles, no longer than 2in (5cm), of other patterns from the wrapping paper to fill in the gaps between the birds.

2 Take the first square of wrapping paper and brush a generous amount of glue all over the back of it.

3 Stick the paper onto the bangle. Then apply a generous amount of glue to your brush and cover the front of the image completely, going over the edges onto the bangle.

4 Add another two pieces of wrapping paper to the bangle and stick down using the glue. Use your finger to smooth the paper down flat and push out any wrinkles. Make sure that all of the paper is stuck to the bangle.

5 Overlap the edges of the bangle with the bird images and fold them around so they stick to the inside. This makes a neat edge and continues the decoration so no gaps show through at all.

6 Keep adding images and glue as above, slightly overlapping them and with some of them diagonal, until every bit of the bangle is covered. Leave to dry completely.

7 Cut four strips from the same sheet of wrapping paper the width of the inside of the bangle and about 2¾in (7cm) in length.

8 Using the same technique as before, stick the strips of paper on the inside of the bangle to cover it completely. Smooth the strips down but don't worry if there a few wrinkles; it is less important on the inside. Leave to dry.

9 Finish with a coat of clear varnish to seal the paper.

Tip *When choosing the wrapping paper images for your bangle, stick to complementary colors, styles, or themes to produce a seamless design.*

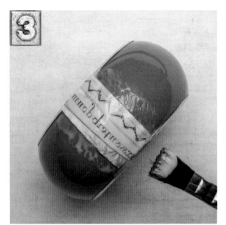

tavi

No one will suspect this darling brooch is made from material for children's craft projects! This is a great way of putting vintage prints to use—make one head scarf for yourself and a mini version for your silhouette brooch.

You will need:

1 Thin foam sheet in black at least 6 x 6in (15 x 15cm)
2 Scraps of vintage fabric
3 Silhouette printed onto paper
4 Pin back

Sticky tape
Nail scissors
Craft glue
Iron

1 Print out a silhouette shape and cut around it, leaving a thin white border.

2 Attach the shape to the foam sheet with sticky tape.

3 Carefully cut around the edge of the silhouette using nail scissors.

4 Repeat the first three steps, so you have two identical foam silhouettes. Glue these together and leave to dry.

5 Cut your vintage fabric into a 12 x 1in (30 x 2.5cm) strip, fold horizontally into three and iron into shape.

6 Wrap the fabric strip around the silhouette's head, tie in a knot or bow and trim off any excess fabric.

7 Turn the silhouette over. Open the pin back, slide the metal bar under the fabric, swing the pin over and close. Secure with a dab of glue.

Tip *You can find foam sheets in most craft stores, and they are dirt cheap!*

trigger

Add some character to your cuffs with these crafty cats. Simple yet very effective, fun cat- and mouse-shape buttons make great novelty cufflinks.

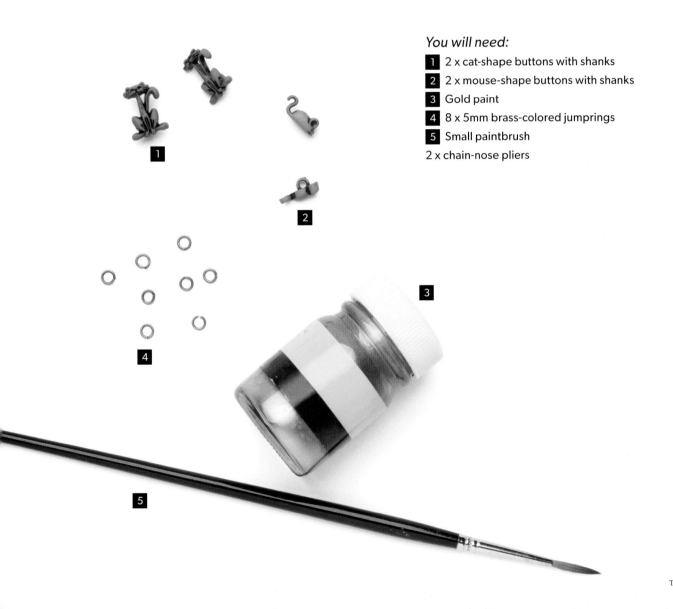

You will need:

1. 2 x cat-shape buttons with shanks
2. 2 x mouse-shape buttons with shanks
3. Gold paint
4. 8 x 5mm brass-colored jumprings
5. Small paintbrush

2 x chain-nose pliers

Tip *If you require a longer section between the buttons then add in extra jumprings.*

1 Take the cat and mouse buttons and coat with the gold paint. Leave to dry.

2 Take the mouse buttons and attach a jumpring (see page 332) to the shank on the back of each one, then close the jumprings.

3 Take another jumpring and attach to the backs of each cat button. Close the jumprings.

4 Attach a second jumpring to the first one on each of the cat buttons and close the jumprings.

5 Attach a second jumpring to each of the closed jumprings on the mouse buttons. Leave these jumprings open.

6 Take the cats and add to the open jumprings on the mouse button. Close the jumprings to finish.

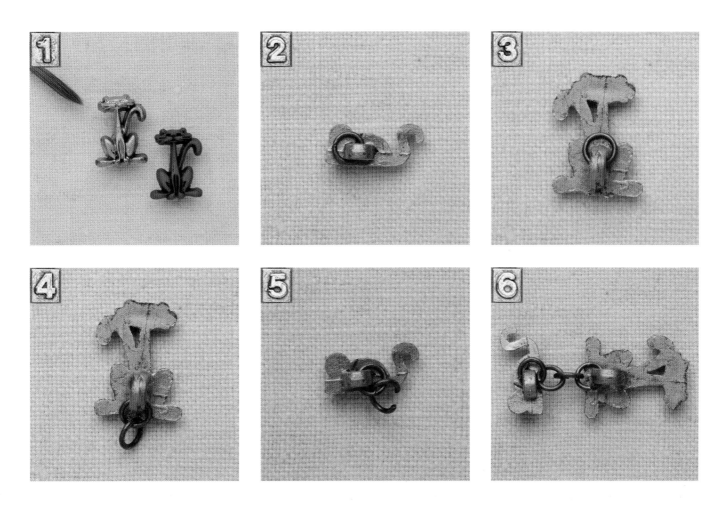

Tip *You could have the cat buttons back-to-back as one cufflink and the two mice together on the other sleeve if you wish.*

amy

This chunky necklace works day or evening, adding a "wow factor" to any outfit. Create this contemporary chain with "Quick Links." They come in various shapes and sizes so you can create your own, unique designs with ease.

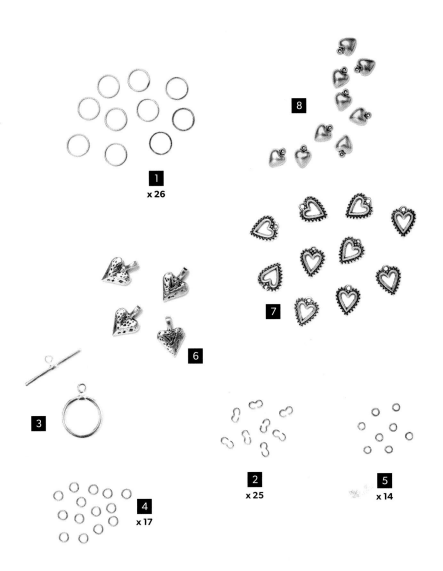

You will need:

1 26 x silver-colored "Quick Links" links

2 25 x silver-colored "Quick Links" connectors

3 1 x silver-colored T-bar and end loop

4 17 x 5mm silver-colored jumprings

5 14 x 4mm silver-colored jumprings

6 4 x large, silver-colored solid heart charms

7 10 x silver-colored open heart charms

8 9 x silver-colored small heart charms

Flat- or snipe-nose pliers

1 x 26

8

7

6

3

2 x 25

5 x 14

4 x 17

1 Take one "Quick Links" link and one connector. Place the link in one side of the connector and, using the pliers, squeeze from the top and bottom of that side of the connector to close and secure the link.

2 Take another "Quick Link", place into the other side of the connector and secure as in step 1.

3 Take another connector and attach to the "Quick Links" already connected from before. Continue to attach all 26 links and 25 connectors together to create the chain. If you would like the necklace to be longer, just continue to add links until you have the length you want.

4 Using the pliers, open one of the 5mm jumprings (see page 332) and thread onto the loop of the T-bar. Attach the jumpring to the last link on one end of the chain. Then add another 5mm jumpring to make sure that the T-bar is securely attached given the weight of the finished necklace. Repeat on the other end of the chain, attaching the catch with two more jumprings.

5 Lay the necklace flat and count 13 links down one side from the catch to find the middle connector.

6 Take the four large solid heart charms and attach and close a 5mm jumpring to each. Then count two links up from

the middle connector of the chain and attach a heart using one of the 4mm jumprings through the 5mm jumpring already attached. Count two links from there and attach another heart. Repeat these two steps on the opposite side of the chain.

7 Take five open heart charms and starting from the middle connector attach one charm with a 4mm jumpring to each empty link. Repeat as a mirror image on the other side of the chain.

8 Take one small heart and use a 5mm jumpring to attach around the middle connector. Attach four small hearts with 5mm jumprings to the next four connectors alongside one side of the chain. Repeat as a mirror image on the opposite side of the chain.

Tip *When the chain is laid flat, imagine the links have two halves—one facing inside and one facing outside. Always attach the charm to the outside of the link so all the charms will hang equally.*

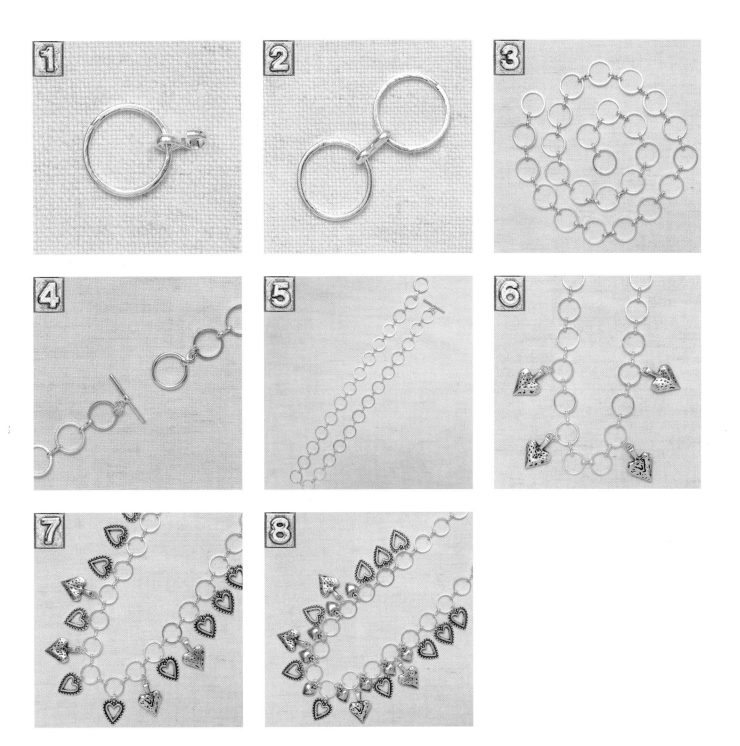

tembo

You'll want to blow your own trumpet when you've made this beautiful bracelet inspired by the majestic African elephant! Using assorted carved wooden beads in multiple rows gives this bracelet a real African vibe.

You will need:

1. 4 x 40mm wooden separators
2. 8 x 14mm elephant beads
3. 4 x 10mm brown feature beads
4. 24 x assorted black-and-white carved wooden beads
5. Roll of beading elastic

Ruler

Scissors

Bead mat

1 To make a bracelet to comfortably fit an average adult's wrist you will need to have enough beads to line up over 7½in (19cm). Start by laying your beads out along a ruler's edge, so you can obtain an even pattern as well as knowing how many beads you will need to reach the required length. We have used 12 assorted beads for each length of elastic.

2 Cut three 15in (38cm) lengths of beading elastic from the roll. It's good to cut the lengths a little longer than required because it makes them easier to tie together at the end.

3 Take your first piece of elastic and thread your beads directly onto it in the same formation as you planned in step 1.

4 Thread your remaining pieces of elastic in the same way. When they are all threaded, check that now they are all beaded they are still all the same length.

5 When all the beads are threaded on, simply tie the corresponding ends together in a double knot and cut off the excess elastic ³⁄₁₆ in (5mm) away from the knot. Move the elastic around so the knot is hidden inside a bead.

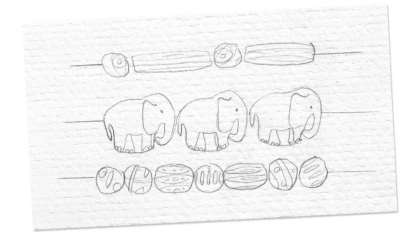

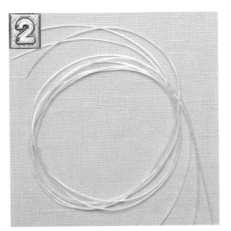

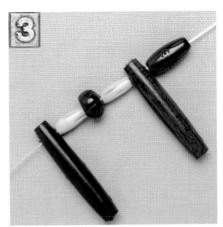

Tip Cut excess elastic slightly away from the knot so it won't unravel through wear. For extra security you can add a drop of superglue.

shari

These stunning earrings will brighten up your day. There are so many beautiful painted beads that feature flowers. These ones look gorgeous hung with a spiral and matching gold beads.

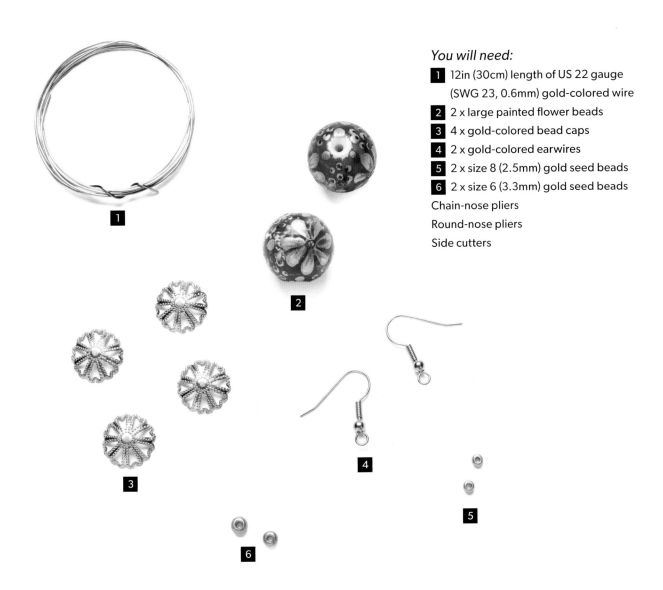

You will need:

1. 12in (30cm) length of US 22 gauge (SWG 23, 0.6mm) gold-colored wire
2. 2 x large painted flower beads
3. 4 x gold-colored bead caps
4. 2 x gold-colored earwires
5. 2 x size 8 (2.5mm) gold seed beads
6. 2 x size 6 (3.3mm) gold seed beads

Chain-nose pliers
Round-nose pliers
Side cutters

1 Cut the 12in (30cm) piece of wire in half and make a spiral at one end on each piece (see page 334).

2 Thread on the size 8 seed bead, a bead cap, the large bead, a bead cap, and the size 6 seed bead.

3 Make a wrapped loop at the top of the wire (see page 337).

4 Open the loop on the earwire and add it to the wrapped loop.

5 Close the earwire loop to finish. Make the second earring in the same way.

Tip *An alternative style can be made by using a headpin instead of the spiral wire. Simply add all the beads and attach to an earwire.*

Tip *This design also works well made with a flat bead and hung on a chain as a pendant.*

romance

You can almost smell the roses when you make this ring! Once you have mastered this easy technique for making a perfect rose, you can use them for brooches, hairbands, and corsages, too. Felt is the ideal fabric as the edges won't fray and it is available in lots of bright colors.

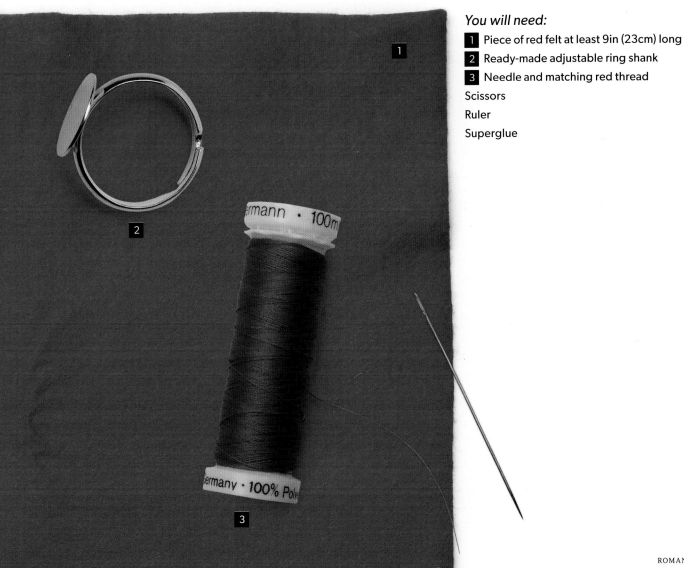

You will need:

1 Piece of red felt at least 9in (23cm) long
2 Ready-made adjustable ring shank
3 Needle and matching red thread
Scissors
Ruler
Superglue

Tip *When cutting your scallops, it doesn't matter if they are not exactly even—the finished rose will just look more natural!*

1 Measure and cut a strip of felt 9in (23cm) long by ¾in (2cm) wide.

2 Measure the halfway point along one of the short sides, then starting at this point, cut a tapered strip from the long side of the felt.

3 Cut deep scallops along the length of the tapered edge.

4 Starting at the narrow end, begin to roll the strip of felt. After two or three turns, put a stitch through the roll to hold it together.

5 Continue to roll the strip and, as you roll, continue to stitch through the layers of felt. From the front you will be able to see the rose taking shape.

6 When you get to the end, secure the end of the strip to the roll with a couple of stitches. Cut off any excess thread.

7 From the front, gently pull the petals open to make a pleasing rose shape.

8 Apply superglue to the ring base. Press the ring base firmly against the back of the rose and allow to dry completely.

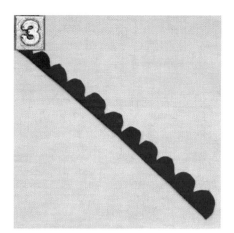

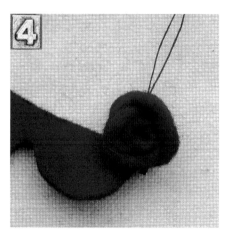

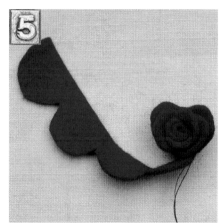

Tip *Try to avoid making the roll for the rose too tight or you will not be able to open out the petals at the end.*

flapper

Get ready to do the Charleston with this jazz-age, Art Deco headdress, which is gorgeous worn forward on the forehead, particularly with a lovely swinging hairdo or fluffy curly bob.

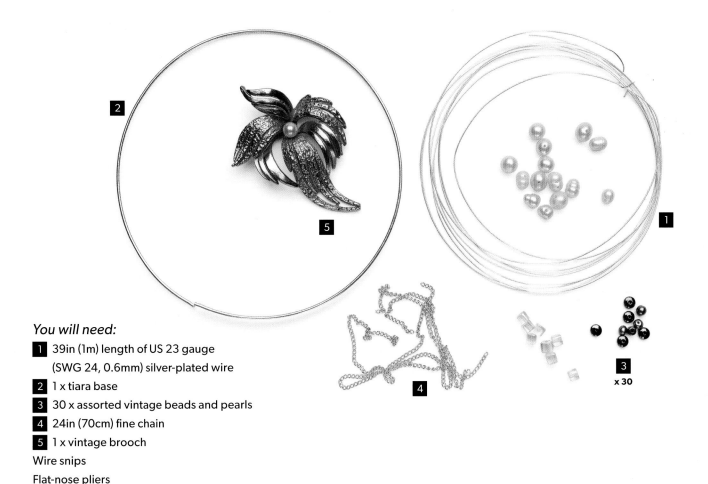

You will need:

1 39in (1m) length of US 23 gauge (SWG 24, 0.6mm) silver-plated wire

2 1 x tiara base

3 30 x assorted vintage beads and pearls

4 24in (70cm) fine chain

5 1 x vintage brooch

Wire snips

Flat-nose pliers

Nail or needle file

Superglue

Iron

Tip *For a slinky bridal look, attach net under the brooch and take it across the head to the other side so it sits snugly over a shiny bob.*

1 Cut a length of wire 16in (40cm) long and at its middle point, wrap it three times around the tiara base about 2in (5cm) from one end.

2 Thread about eight beads onto one of the loose wire ends, then carefully curve the wire over the headdress following the shape of the tiara base. This wire should sit to one side of the base; wrap the wire around the base 2in (5cm) from the other end.

3 Add eight or nine beads to the other long end of wire, ease it to the other side of the band and wrap it at the same point as before: don't cut off the excess wire yet as you can use it to attach the brooch and chain.

4 Attach another 16in (40cm) long piece of wire to the tiara, starting on the opposite end to before. Add the rest of the beads as before, dividing them unequally between the two ends of wire. Ease the wires over to the other side of the headdress so that they sit either side of the first bead-laden lengths of wire. Wrap these at the opposite side as before.

5 Snip three varied lengths of chain for each side and thread them onto one of the loose ends of wire. Wrap the wire around the base to hold them in place. On one side, trim the second wire neatly and squeeze with the pliers (see page 341).

6 Prepare your vintage brooch by carefully cutting off the pin and filing down any sharp edges. Firmly wire the brooch into your chosen position using the remaining end of wire. Trim off any excess wire and squeeze the end flat with the pliers.

7 To finish off, carefully dot glue at random points on the long pieces of wire and gently push the beads into place. Leave the headdress upright so that the glue can dry while you fix your cocktail.

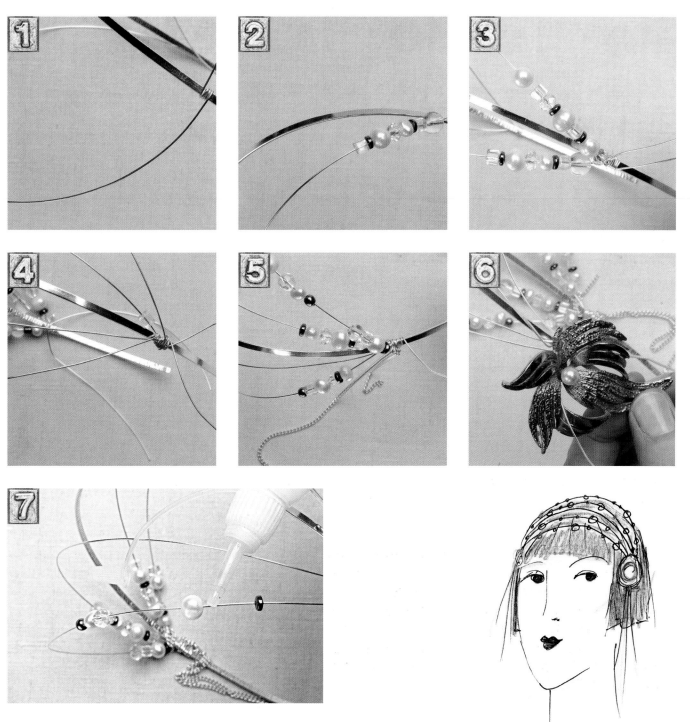

clusters

You can group beads in a different way to create clusters or bunches—this technique lends itself to a whole variety of possibilities. As well as grapes, you could make blackberries or raspberries, or simply a mix of beads.

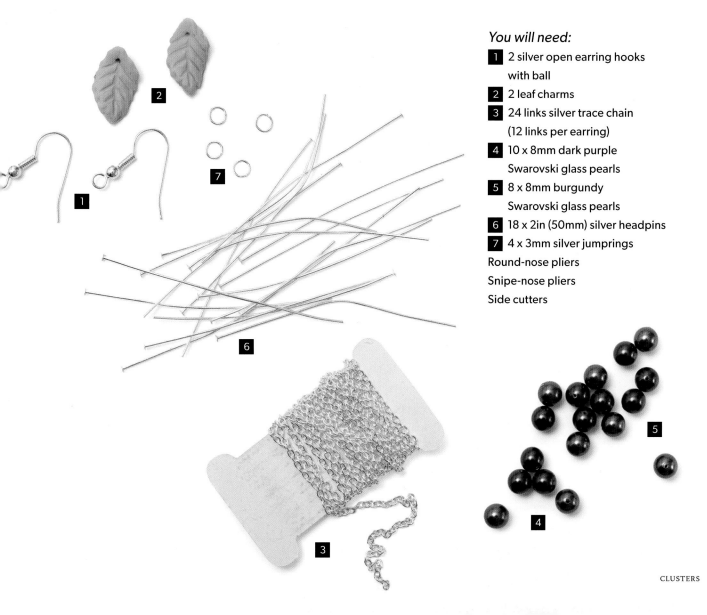

You will need:

1. 2 silver open earring hooks with ball
2. 2 leaf charms
3. 24 links silver trace chain (12 links per earring)
4. 10 x 8mm dark purple Swarovski glass pearls
5. 8 x 8mm burgundy Swarovski glass pearls
6. 18 x 2in (50mm) silver headpins
7. 4 x 3mm silver jumprings

Round-nose pliers

Snipe-nose pliers

Side cutters

1 Open the loop on an earring hook, thread on 12 links of silver chain and close.

2 Thread a 2in (50mm) headpin through a glass pearl and make a hook, leaving the headpin length intact.

3 Pass the headpin length through the last link of chain.

4 Holding onto the top of the hook with snipe nose pliers, wrap the long end of the wire around itself a couple of times. This will create a small spiral of wire on top of the pearl. Cut off any excess headpin.

5 Repeat steps 2–4 until you have threaded nine pearls (5 x dark purple and 4 x burgundy) randomly onto the length of chain.

6 Open a 3mm jumpring, thread a leaf onto it and close.

7 Open another 3mm jumpring, thread this through the loop on the earring hook and the jumpring holding the leaf, then close.

8 Finally, repeat the process to create the other earring.

Tip *The key to making these earrings look like bunches of grapes is to cluster more beads at the top of the chain and fewer at the bottom.*

Variation *This technique is very similar to making the grapes. The difference is that you can use any shaped beads or colors you want.*

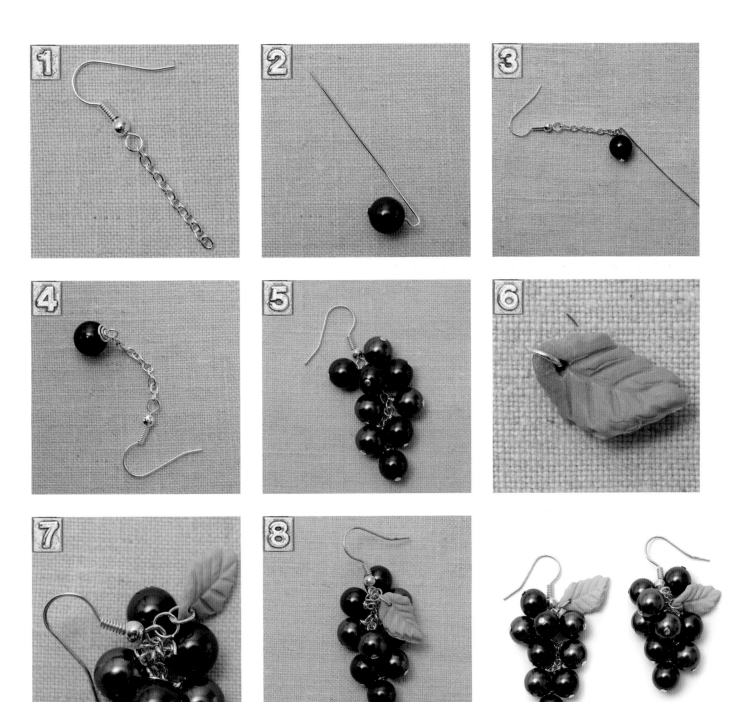

pearly

A beautiful bird's nest, especially when filled with tiny eggs, is a symbol of hope, love, nurture, and protection. The key to this design is the delicate nature of the nest, so you'll need to work carefully to achieve the right look.

You will need:

1 60in (1.5m) length of US 26 gauge (SWG 27, 0.4mm) brass wire

2 12in (30cm) length of US 20 gauge (SWG 21, 0.8mm) brass wire

3 3 x pearl beads

Snipe-nose or flat-nose pliers

End cutters

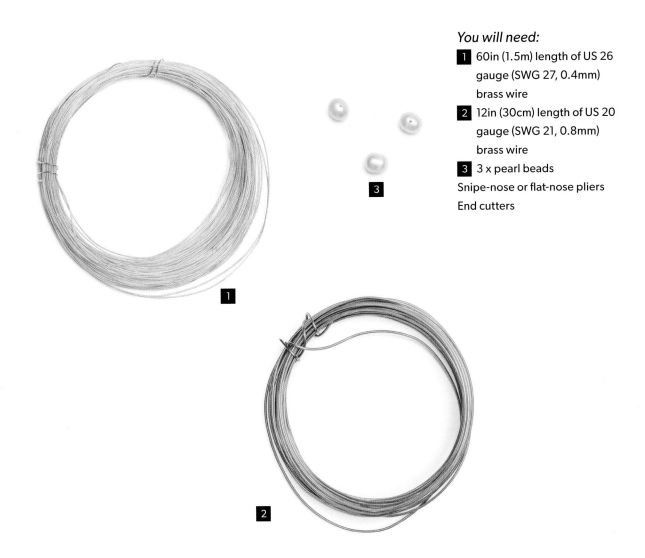

1 Thread the three pearl beads onto one end of the US 26 gauge (SWG 27, 0.4mm) wire and about 8in (20cm) along the length. Push the pearls together into a triangle and twist the two ends tightly together three times. This will leave you with one really long end and one shorter end of wire.

2 Using your fingers, make kinks along the whole length of the long end. Next, wrap this long end of wire closely around the edge of the pearls in a circle. You will have to hold onto the wire as you form the circles as they will want to spring out of shape! Wrap it around the pearls at least five times.

3 Thread the long end under the nest and up through the middle but to the left of the pearls. Wrap the wire around in this place twice more.

Tip *Use pliers to wrap the loops around the wire so you can pull the loops tight and keep them close together.*

Make a half circle with the wire around to the opposite side of the nest and repeat the threading.

4 Turn the nest over and, again with the long end of wire, wrap it around in circles of different sizes until the bottom is covered and you are left with a piece approximately 7in (18cm) long.

5 Thread this end over the top of the nest and down through the center, making sure to go through the circle of wire attached to the pearls, and wrap again like this twice more. Repeat on the opposite side of the nest. Do these wraps away from those in step 3 to secure the nest in four different places.

6 Find the center of the US 20 gauge (SWG 21, 0.8mm) wire, rest it on your chosen finger, and wind each end of the wire once around your finger to make three loops.

7 Take the wire off your finger. Take one end of wire and, using your pliers, wrap it around all three loops tightly, twice. Using the end cutters, snip off the excess wire and tuck the end neatly against the wraps. Repeat with the other side of the wire.

8 Place the nest on top of the ring in the middle of the wraps and hold in place. Using the excess wire on the nest, thread it in between two of the loops in the ring and up through the middle of the nest and back around but in between the other two loops the second time. Keep going until the wire is all used and tuck the end into the nest.

9 Repeat on the opposite side of the ring.

polly

Keep your beloved pet always close by with this lovely portrait necklace.
Pendant blanks and glass cabochons make creating a beautiful personalized
pendant really easy.

1

3

2

4

You will need:

1 1 x 1in (25mm) square silver-colored
    pendant blank

2 1 x 1in (25mm) square glass
    cabochon

3 1 x cat picture

4 1 x finished necklace chain

White (PVA) glue

Glue brush

Superglue

Small sharp scissors

Pencil

Ruler

Sticky tack

1 Print a photo of the cat; you'll need the image to be at least 1in (25mm) in size. Use the glass cabochon to select the part of the image you want to feature in the pendant.

2 Hold the cabochon in place and mark all four sides with a pencil. Don't draw all the way around as the cabochon's corners are slightly rounded and you need a sharp square edge.

3 Take the ruler and line it up with your marks from step 2, then draw in the complete lines so they cross over in the corners. Cut the shape out with sharp-pointed scissors.

4 Take the white (PVA) glue and coat the picture. Make sure you coat both sides and go right over the edges. Do this in two steps, allowing the first side to dry before turning over to coat the other side. This will stop the superglue from soaking into the paper and spoiling the pendant.

5 When you are sure the picture is completely dry, place a small drop of superglue in the pendant and place the picture over the top. Smooth over the picture to make sure the glue spreads out. Allow to completely dry.

6 Place another couple of drops of superglue on the picture and place the glass cabochon on top. With a piece of sticky tack, push down firmly on the glass cabochon—this will force any air bubbles out from under the glass and will also spread the glue out to an even, thin coat. Hold until you are sure the glue will stay in place, then leave the tack on the glass until the pendant has completely dried.

7 Take the tack off the glass and thread the chain through the pendant bail to finish.

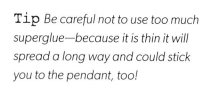

Tip *Be careful not to use too much superglue—because it is thin it will spread a long way and could stick you to the pendant, too!*

Tip *Pendant blanks come in lots of different shapes and finishes so pick the style that suits you the best. You could attach it to a keyring if you prefer.*

canary

These delightful bird-on-a-perch charms will look stunning with a little black dress and add style to casual jeans and a T-shirt. The clever design allows you to add extra charms within them, too. Swarovski crystal beads have been used here to add sparkle.

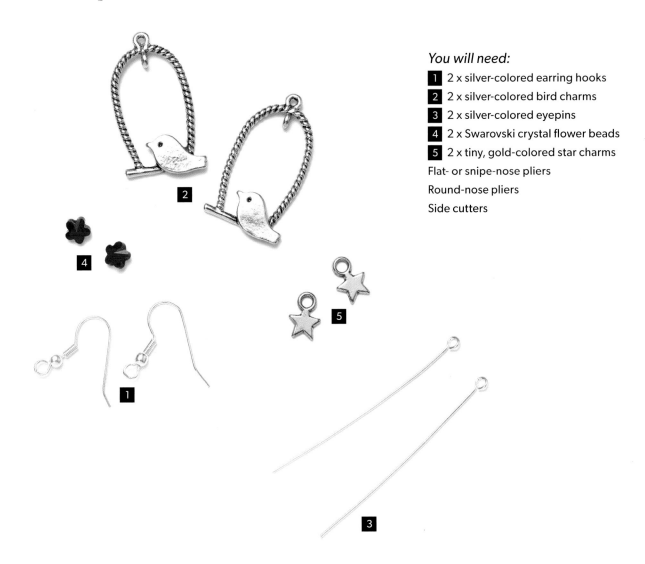

You will need:

1. 2 x silver-colored earring hooks
2. 2 x silver-colored bird charms
3. 2 x silver-colored eyepins
4. 2 x Swarovski crystal flower beads
5. 2 x tiny, gold-colored star charms

Flat- or snipe-nose pliers

Round-nose pliers

Side cutters

1 Using the flat- or snipe-nose pliers, open the loop at the bottom of the earring hook (the same way you open a jumpring—see page 332) and thread through the top loop of the bird charm.

2 Take an eyepin and thread on the Swarovski flower bead to the end of the pin. Using the pliers, bend the wire as close to the top of the bead as possible at a 90-degree angle to the bead, with the loop of the eyepin on its side (see page 336).

3 Holding onto the existing loop with the flat- or snipe-nose pliers, use the round-nose pliers to create another loop in the pin, facing the opposite direction to the existing loop. Snip off the excess wire using the side cutters but do not close the loop.

4 Thread the star charm onto the open loop and close the loop using the flat- or snipe-nose pliers.

5 Open the other loop above the bead and thread onto the solid loop inside the bird charm.

6 Now repeat step 1 with the matching earring but this time turn the bird charm around to face the opposite direction. Repeat steps 2 to 5.

Tip *Earrings always look best when they are a mirror image of each other because they balance and complement the face.*

knotty

This necklace is great as there is no need for any findings at all—the beads are all that matter! To play on the knotting theme, choose beads that are all made from knots and cord. Try to keep the distance between each bead the same.

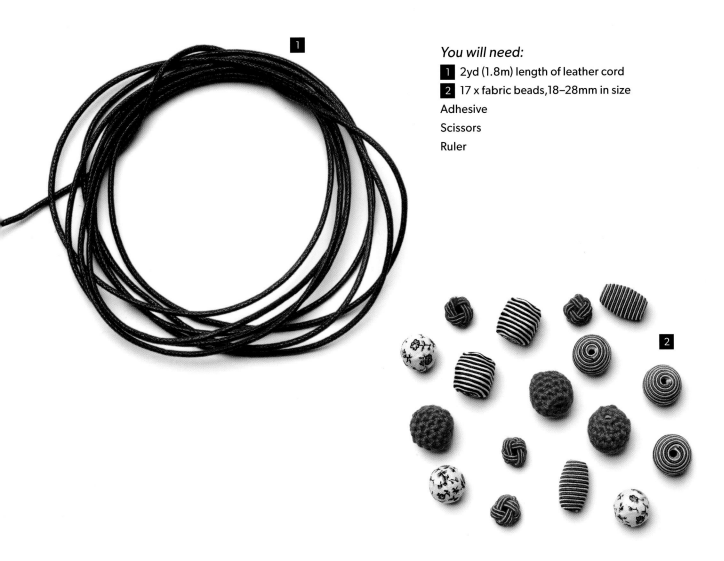

You will need:

1 2yd (1.8m) length of leather cord
2 17 x fabric beads, 18–28mm in size
Adhesive
Scissors
Ruler

1 At one end of the leather cord, make a loop large enough for one of your beads to pass through. When you have made the loop the right size, tie a knot in the cord to secure the loop size and set the bead to one side. Cut away the excess cord ½in (1cm) from the knot. Apply a drop of adhesive to the knot and wrap the short end of the cord around the long length to finish the knot off neatly.

2 Lay your cord against a ruler and tie a knot approximately 2¾in (7cm) along from your knotted loop.

3 Slide the first bead along the leather cord until it rests on the knot you have just made. Tie another knot directly after the bead to hold it in place on the cord.

4 Tie another knot 1¼in (3cm) along the leather cord from the bead. Add another bead, slide it along to meet this knot and tie another knot directly after it.

5 Continue tying knots and adding beads until there is only the one bead left that fitted the loop you made in step 1. Add this final bead and place it on the leather cord 2¾in (7cm) along from the last bead.

6 Take the end of the leather cord and tie a knot under the final bead to secure it in place. As in step 1, cut away the excess cord ½in (1cm) from the knot. Apply a drop of adhesive to the knot and wrap the short end of the cord around the long length to finish the knot off neatly.

Tip *Lay out all your beads first to calculate how long you want to make your necklace and determine the length of leather cord between each bead.*

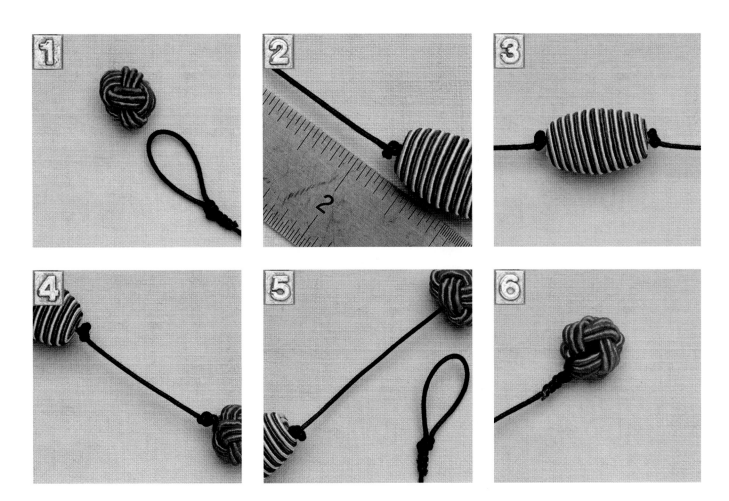

Tip *Adding a drop of adhesive to the end of your leather cord sets it hard, so that it is easy to thread through the beads.*

gecko

Use the art of beading to give the classic 1920s' lizard brooch a modern twist!
To get a great geometric, scaly skin effect use bicone crystals rather than
seed beads for this animal pattern.

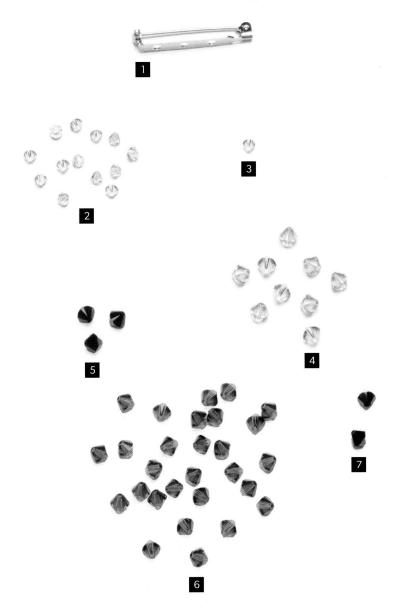

You will need:

1   1 x sew-on brooch pin

2   13 x 4mm light topaz bicone crystals

3   1 x 4mm peridot bicone crystal

4   9 x 6mm peridot bicone crystals

5   3 x 6mm light siam bicone crystals

6   28 x 6mm emerald bicone crystals

7   2 x 6mm jet bicone crystals

8   39in (1m) length of US 28 gauge (SWG 30, 0.3mm) green beading wire

Side cutters

Needle

Green cotton thread

Scissors

1 If you have done bead work before then you can use the bead map illustrated right. Alternatively, thread one emerald bead halfway along the length of green beading wire. Bend the wire down either side of the bead so you have a left wire and a right wire of equal length. Add two emerald beads onto the left wire then thread the right wire through both beads in the opposite direction. Pull the wire so the three beads come together to form a small triangle.

2 Onto the left wire add: one jet bead, one emerald bead, and another jet bead. Again, thread the right wire through all three beads in the opposite direction and pull. You now have six beads all together in a triangle formation.

3 Thread onto the left wire two emerald beads and once more take the right wire and thread through both these two beads going in the opposite direction. Pull the wire to bring all the beads together to form the head.

4 Take the left wire and thread on two emerald beads followed by three light topaz beads. Then thread the wire back through the two emerald beads going the other way. Gently pull the wire and you have formed one leg. Repeat this step to make the other leg on the right-hand wire.

5 Add beads onto the left wire as follows: one emerald bead followed by one light siam bead, followed by a further emerald bead. Again, take the right wire and thread through all three beads going the opposite way and pull. This is now the first line of the body.

6 Keep adding the following formations onto the left wire and then threading the right wire back through the beads each time. For the next row, thread: one emerald bead, two larger peridot beads, and one emerald bead. For the following row thread: one larger peridot bead, one light siam bead, and one larger peridot bead. For the next row use: one emerald bead, two larger peridot beads, and one emerald bead. For the final body row, thread: one emerald bead, one light siam bead, and a last emerald bead.

7 Now the body is formed you need to make the other two legs. In the same way as you made the previous legs, thread on two emerald beads followed by three light topaz beads on the left wire. Then thread the wire

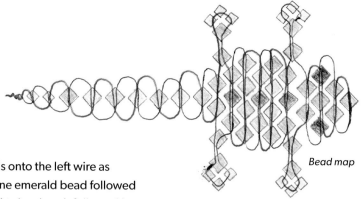

Bead map

back through the two emerald beads going the other way. Repeat again to make the other leg on the right-hand wire.

8 Take two emerald beads and thread them onto the left wire. Again, thread the right wire through both beads going in the opposite direction and pull so the beads fit snugly together.

9 To make the tail add onto the left wire one emerald bead and then thread the right wire through the bead the opposite way. Continue this process, alternating the emerald and larger peridot beads until they are all used. Now add the small peridot bead onto the left wire, threading the right wire through it the opposite way and finally the last light topaz b ead. Twist the wires together, thread them back through the light topaz bead, and cut away excess wire. Sew the brooch pin onto the back using green cotton.

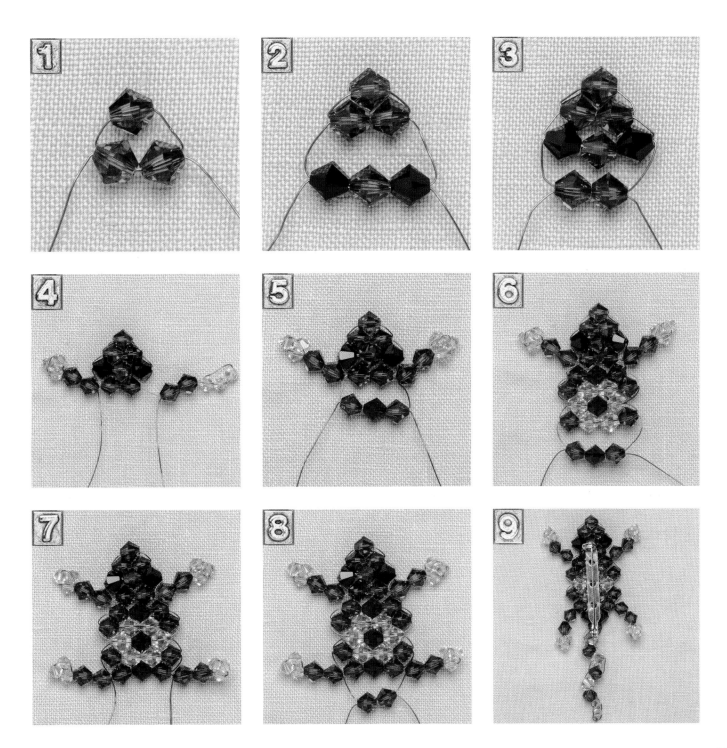

emma

A funky hair grip, perfect for a summer party. Pretty flowers and beautiful beads attached to a hair grip by lengths of chain create a delightful decoration that is as fun to wear as it is to make.

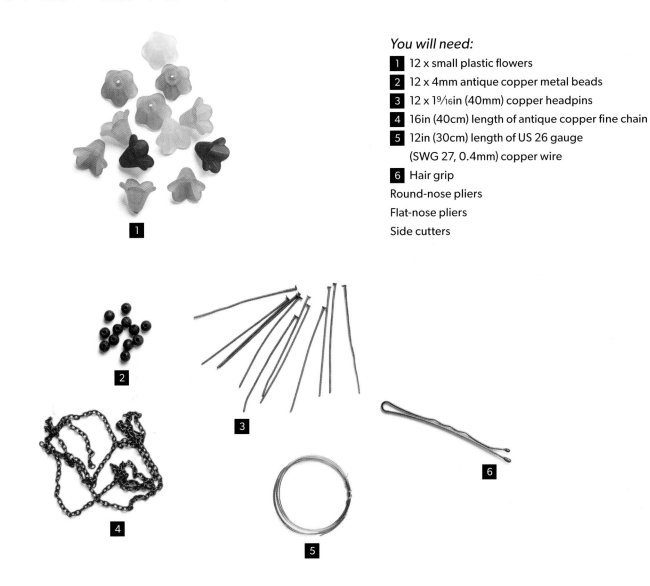

You will need:

1. 12 x small plastic flowers
2. 12 x 4mm antique copper metal beads
3. 12 x 1⁹⁄₁₆in (40mm) copper headpins
4. 16in (40cm) length of antique copper fine chain
5. 12in (30cm) length of US 26 gauge (SWG 27, 0.4mm) copper wire
6. Hair grip

Round-nose pliers

Flat-nose pliers

Side cutters

1 Thread a copper bead then a flower onto a headpin. Make five more.

2 Start to make a wrapped loop (see page 337), but before you finish the loop, open it slightly and thread on a 3½in (9cm) length of chain. Finish the wrapped loop. Repeat for the other five headpins, attaching to chains reducing in length by ⅜in (10mm) each time.

3 Make up the other six flowers in the same way but don't add any chain. Place to one side.

4 Take the US 26-gauge (SWG 27, 0.4mm) wire and place it on the hair grip. Twist the ends together to secure the wire.

5 Thread on all six chains and twist the wire around the end of the grip to secure the chains.

6 Thread on a flower made in step 3 and twist the wire around the grip again. Go through the loop of the flower twice to hold it in place. Add another flower and do the same. Add a third flower and wrap the wire around all three flowers to hold them securely. Add the other three flowers around the outside, wrapping the wire around a couple of times in between adding the flowers. Finish by wrapping the wire around the hair grip a couple of times and cut off any excess.

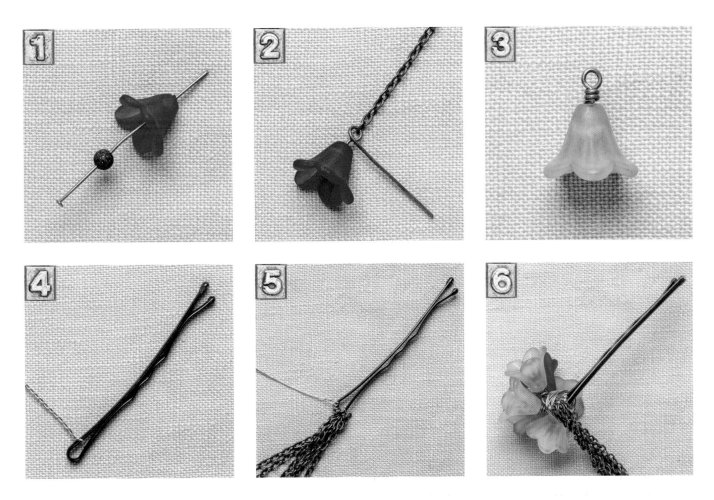

Tip *An alternative design would be to make a bigger cluster on the grip without any hanging chains.*

jan

Charm and elegance are combined in this pretty item. Add a fancy clasp onto a small piece of an enamel necklace and link it with a leather cord to create a fabulous bracelet.

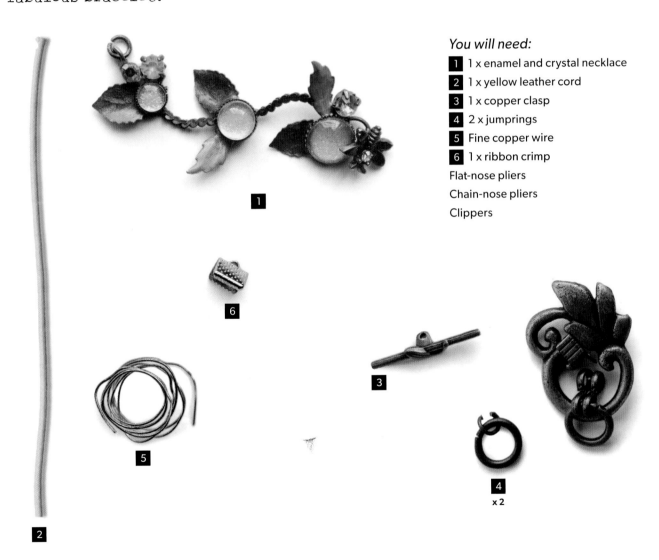

You will need:

1 1 x enamel and crystal necklace
2 1 x yellow leather cord
3 1 x copper clasp
4 2 x jumprings
5 Fine copper wire
6 1 x ribbon crimp
Flat-nose pliers
Chain-nose pliers
Clippers

x 2

1 Lay out the necklace to decide which piece would work best for making the bracelet. Make sure that this piece has ends that can be linked to jumprings. Clip off the section you have chosen using wire clippers. Keep the clippers sharp by snipping emery paper a few times. The glass grit will help to keep the clippers in top condition.

2 Measure your wrist and add 1³⁄₁₆in (30mm) to the length. Lay the piece on the tape measure to calculate how much leather cord is needed. Cut a piece of cord twice the required length. Then cut a chain half as long.

3 Fold the cord in half, then crimp the cut ends together with a ribbon crimp (see attaching a cord end page 340). Link the wire-wrapped end of cord to the clasp toggle with a jumpring. Attach the chain to the same jumpring, then use chain-nose and flat-nose pliers to close it securely.

4 To create a neat loop at the other end of the cord, squeeze the two lengths together and firmly wrap them a large crimp bead or fine copper wire (snip off the excess wire with clippers). Link this end to one end of the jewelry piece and to the other end of the chain with another jumpring.

5 Attach a clasp to the other end of the bracelet with the remaining jumpring.

Tip *Save any extra pieces to make earrings and a matching necklace. Store them in a small organza bag to keep them safe.*

effloresce

This pretty flower trim is easily snipped into individual "blossoms." The pastel colors suit the spring blossoms theme but flowers of one color would look great, too.

You will need:

1 Flower trim/lace—approximately 12in (30cm) depending on the design

2 15 x 3mm round beads or faux pearls

3 Short length of 3/16in (5mm)-wide white elastic (see step 1 overleaf for exact length needed)

Needle and thread

Sharp scissors

1 Measure your finger and cut a piece of elastic to the right size, plus about ¾in (2cm). Stitch through both layers ⅜in (1cm) from the end. Trim one end close to the stitches.

2 Fold the longer end around the short and tuck both cut ends inward. Stitch through all the layers to hide the rough ends.

3 Divide the trim by carefully snipping between the flowers.

4 Stitch through the elastic, the center of the first flower, one of the beads and then back through the center of the flower.

5 Make a couple of stitches along the elastic then add two more flowers with beads, side by side. Continue alternating single and then double rows of flowers, which will give your ring a full and flowery appearance.

6 Continue stitching flowers and beads around the ring, cutting more if needed. When you reach the end, secure the thread on the reverse with a couple of extra stitches and trim the end neatly.

Tip *The cut ends of elastic will quickly fray so it is worth spending a few minutes hiding them neatly.*

buttons

There is not much that can beat the fantastic variety of both antique and modern button shapes and colors. When using recycled buttons you may struggle to find two exactly the same. Play on this idea in your designs.

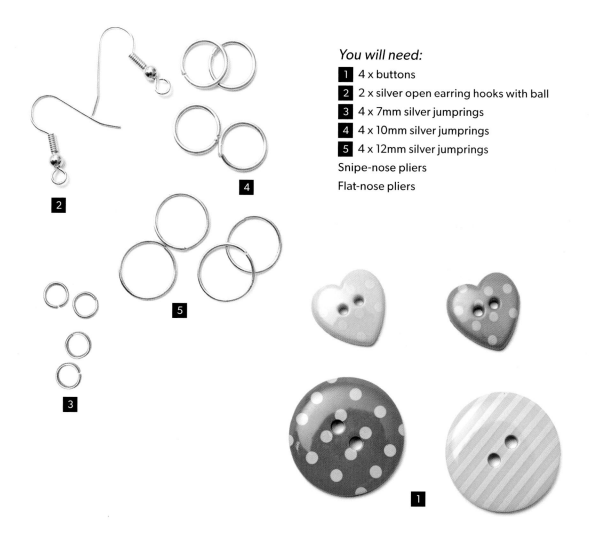

You will need:

1 4 x buttons

2 2 x silver open earring hooks with ball

3 4 x 7mm silver jumprings

4 4 x 10mm silver jumprings

5 4 x 12mm silver jumprings

Snipe-nose pliers

Flat-nose pliers

1 Open a 10mm jumpring, thread it onto the left hole of the heart button and close.

2 Open another 10mm jumpring, thread it onto the right hole of the same heart button and close.

3 Open a 12mm jumpring, thread it through the left hole of the large round button and close.

4 Open a 12mm jumpring, thread it through the right hole of the same button and close.

5 Open a 7mm jumpring, link it through the two 10mm jumprings at the top of the heart and through one of the 12mm jumprings on the large round button, then close.

6 Open another 7mm jumpring, link it through the other 12mm jumpring on the large round button and through the eye loop on an earring hook and close.

7 Finally, repeat the process to create the other earring.

Tip *This design will look fantastic using vintage buttons and antique silver chain and findings. Why not give it a go?*

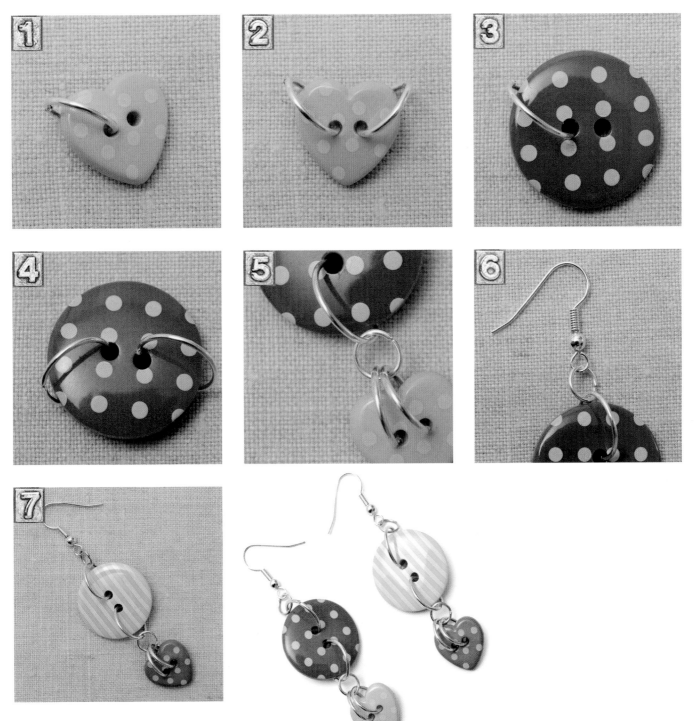

scoubidou

The way you plait and knot leather and suede cords can create many different patterns. This design is based on the fad called scoubidou, which originally used thin plastic tubes, but here it has lengths of suede to give it a modern twist.

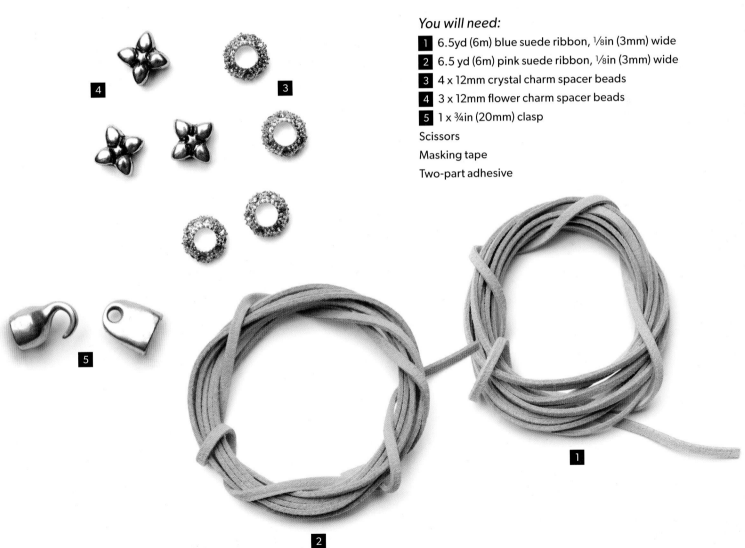

You will need:

1. 6.5yd (6m) blue suede ribbon, 1/8in (3mm) wide
2. 6.5 yd (6m) pink suede ribbon, 1/8in (3mm) wide
3. 4 x 12mm crystal charm spacer beads
4. 3 x 12mm flower charm spacer beads
5. 1 x 3/4in (20mm) clasp

Scissors

Masking tape

Two-part adhesive

1 Cut your lengths of ribbon in half, so you have 2 x 3.3yd (3m) lengths of each color. Holding the four lengths at one end, wrap a little piece of masking tape around the ends to hold them all together. Then holding the masking taped ends, fan the suede lengths out to form a cross shape, ensuring the colors alternate.

2 Working in a clockwise direction, loop the top pink length of suede over the length of blue suede to its right.

3 Take this blue length of suede and loop it over the bottom pink length.

4 Then take this pink length and loop it over the blue length of suede to its left.

5 Finally take this last blue length and thread it through the loop you made with the first pink length of suede in step 2.

6 Pull all four lengths of suede and they will come together tightly to form a small neat square of alternating colors.

7 Repeat steps 2–6 over and over, so that you start to form a tight spiral of suede. When you have built up a length of 2in (5cm), thread all four lengths of suede through the hole of the first crystal charm spacerbead. Slide the bead along the suede until it meets the spiral.

8 Repeat steps 2–6 to create another 2in (5cm) of spiralled suede, then thread all four lengths of suede through the hole on a flower-shaped spacer bead.

9 Repeat steps 7 and 8, alternating crystal charm and flower spacer beads, until you have a 16-in (40cm) spiral of suede with the spacer beads every 2in (5cm). Trim all the suede ends so that they are the same length, wrapping a piece of masking tape around them to temporarily hold them in place. Mix up some two-part adhesive (see page 351) and place it in the ends of the large clasp. Remove the masking tape from each end of the suede and push the suede ends into the clasp and hold until set.

Tip *Use beads with really large holes, so that you can thread them easily over the leather and suede cords.*

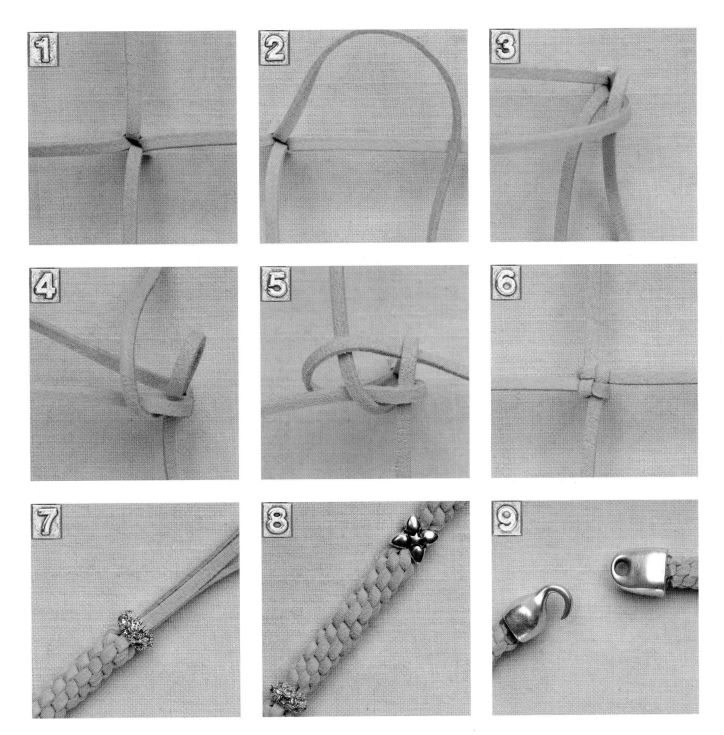

skye

This Victorian drawing of a stag gives these cufflinks a vintage feel and will make that special someone feel like laird of the manor! Make sure you coat your images on both sides in white (PVA) glue so the paper doesn't absorb the resin.

You will need:

1 2 x ¹¹/₁₆in (17mm) square-tray cufflink blanks

2 Pale-colored card

3 Two-part, pour-on, high-gloss resin

White (PVA) glue

Paint brush

Oil-based modeling clay (Plasticine)

Scissors

Mixing pots and sticks

1 Source an image of a stag's head from the Internet and scale it to size so it will fit inside the cufflink blank. Copy the image and then reverse it so you now have a pair of images. Print it out onto the pale colored card.

2 Cut out each image slightly smaller than $^{11}/_{16}$in (17mm) square so that they fit comfortably inside the cufflink blanks. Coat each image with white (PVA) glue back and front, then leave to dry.

3 Stick each image into the base of each cufflink blank, again using a small amount of white glue.

4 Prop each cufflink blank so the tray containing the image is completely horizontal. This is easily done using soft modeling clay, such as Plasticine.

5 High-gloss resins usually come in two parts: the actual resin and the hardener. Following the instructions on the packaging, mix equal parts of each thoroughly and pour the mixture into each tray of the cufflink blanks (see page 352).

6 The consistency is very thick, so you can be generous with the amount you pour in because it does slightly shrink back when it cures. Blow lightly on the surface to pop the larger bubbles and leave to dry thoroughly.

Tip *Think about how to "pair" your chosen images for each cufflink. Simply reverse them for a subtle difference.*

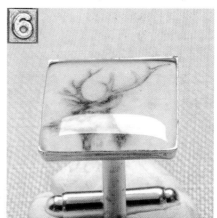

Tip *Any small bubbles in your resin will disappear as it dries out.*

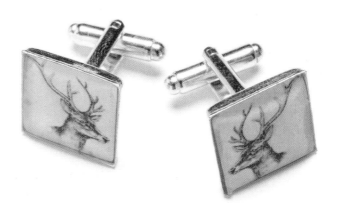

chelsea

Think outside the square and use knitted tubes of wire to link ceramic beads to make a bold statement. Their glassy glaze catches the light, making this the perfect bead for an evening bracelet.

5

4

3
x 10

You will need:

1 Knitted wire tubing
2 6 x ceramic beads
3 10 x 10mm jumprings
4 2 x ribbon crimps
5 1 x parrot clasp with jumpring attached
Short length of chain
Flat-nose pliers
Chain-nose pliers

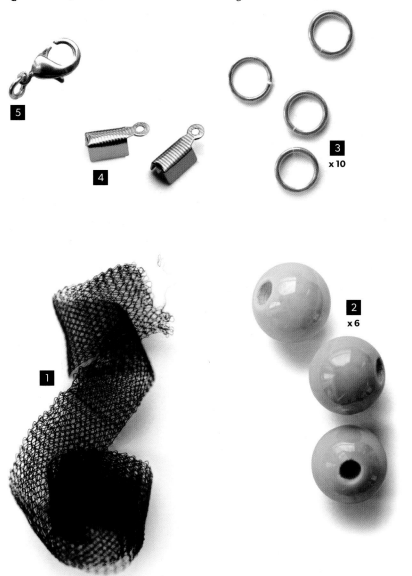

1

2
x 6

1 Measure a length of knitted wire to fit your wrist, adding on an additional 2¾in (7cm) before cutting.

2 Tie a knot in the end of the wire while leaving a small piece extending from the knot. Paint the end of the wire extruding from the knot with clear nail varnish to prevent it unravelling.

3 Using the flat-nose pliers, place this end of the wire in a flat ribbon crimp. Close the crimp securely and give it a gentle tug to ensure that the wire is firmly caught in the crimp.

4 Thread on the beads separated by the silver jumprings. When you have used three beads, tie a loose knot in the center of the wire before continuing with the remainder of the beads.

5 Once all the beads and jumprings have been threaded onto the wire, tie a knot in the end close to the last bead. Trim the wire with scissors, leaving just enough to crimp in the remaining flat crimp. Add a small length of chain to the end of the crimp to act as a bracelet extender.

6 Attach the clasp to the other end of the bracelet. Open the jumpring on the clasp using both the flat-nose and chain-nose pliers. Finally, thread this jumpring through the hole on the end of the crimp and close the ring securely.

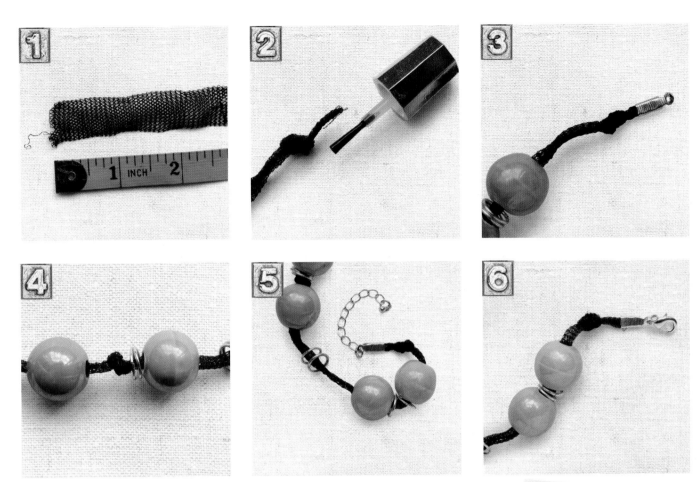

Tip *Knitted wire is fun to work with. It can be filled with beads, twisted into a variety of shapes and comes in many different colors.*

rose

Hearts and flowers adorn this romantic choker. Perfect for Valentine's Day or an anniversary date, this delightful item is trimmed with ribbon roses and tiny heart buttons to give a sophisticated look.

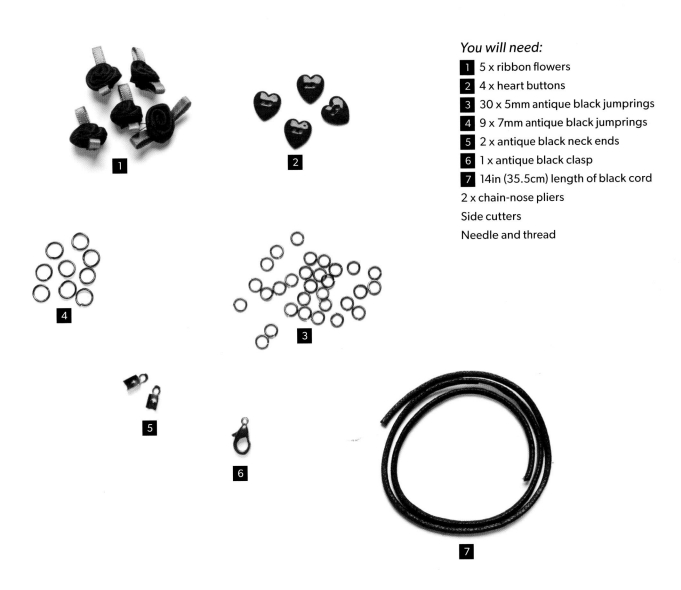

You will need:

1 5 x ribbon flowers
2 4 x heart buttons
3 30 x 5mm antique black jumprings
4 9 x 7mm antique black jumprings
5 2 x antique black neck ends
6 1 x antique black clasp
7 14in (35.5cm) length of black cord
2 x chain-nose pliers
Side cutters
Needle and thread

1 Take a ribbon rose and add a 5mm jumpring to each end (see page 332). Close the jumprings. Repeat for all five ribbon roses.

2 Take a button and attach a 7mm jumpring through both holes. Close the rings and attach both to a 5mm jumpring. Repeat for all four buttons.

3 Thread the roses onto the cord, going through the jumprings from the front so they sit on the cord as they appear in the step image. Thread on all five.

4 Take a 5mm jumpring and thread through the 5mm jumprings between two roses, attaching them together. Add a button before closing the ring.

5 Center the rose chain on the cord. To make sure it doesn't move when wearing, take a length of thread and sew the end jumprings to the cord.

6 Add a neck end to the ends of the cord (see page 340). Add four 5mm jumprings to each neck end. Add the clasp to the final 5mm jumpring on one side; add the final 7mm jumpring to the other side.

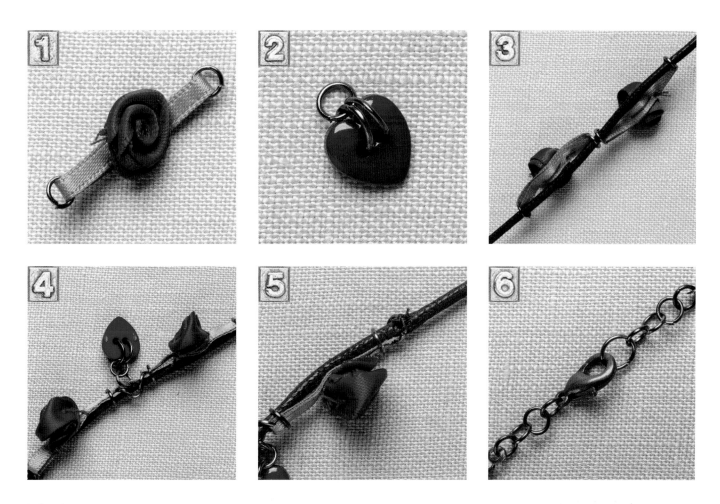

Tip *Ribbon roses come in all sorts of colors. This necklace would look great in any color but just make sure you buy ones with ribbon loops to take the jumprings.*

luster

This ring will introduce you to two basic crochet stitches. Once you have mastered these you will be able to rustle up ring after ring with ease. Crochet is a simple, traditional craft that requires no more than a hook and a ball of yarn. The addition of some sequins and crystals brings this ring up to date.

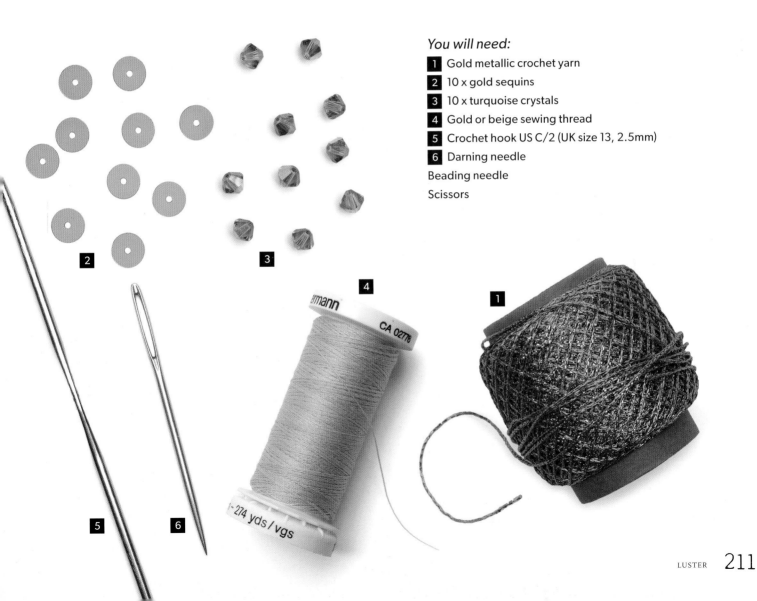

You will need:
1 Gold metallic crochet yarn
2 10 x gold sequins
3 10 x turquoise crystals
4 Gold or beige sewing thread
5 Crochet hook US C/2 (UK size 13, 2.5mm)
6 Darning needle
Beading needle
Scissors

1 Measure around your finger with a piece of yarn and cut to size. This will be your guide for the circumference of the ring. Create a crochet chain to the same length as the guide (see page 342).

2 Join the chain into a ring by hooking the yarn through the first chain stitch. Make two more chain stitches to raise the yarn to the level of the next row.

3 Using double crochet stitch (see page 343), work around the ring, inserting the hook into the center of the ring to begin each new stitch.

4 When the first row is complete, join the last stitch to the first with a simple chain stitch. Then make two more chain stitches to raise the yarn to the level of the second row.

5 Work a second row of double crochet, hooking into the space between each stitch in the first row of stitches.

6 At the end of the second row, join the last stitch to the first with a chain stitch. Cut the yarn, leaving a tail of about 4in (10cm). Push the tail through the last loop and pull up tightly to secure.

7 Use a darning needle to loosely stitch the tail ends of the yarn into the main body of the ring and trim any excess. This should hide and secure the ends of the yarn.

8 Use the beading needle and sewing thread to sew the sequins and crystals around the ring in a random pattern.

Tip *Don't worry if your ring looks flat rather than round in the early stages, the shape will come together as you add more rows.*

Tip *Keep the stitches in the initial chain fairly tight or your finished ring will end up being much larger than expected.*

leandri

These lava rock pebbles are as light as a feather. Combined with coiled wire links, they create a very feminine piece with a modern edge. Hammering the wire coils is also a great stress-busting activity!

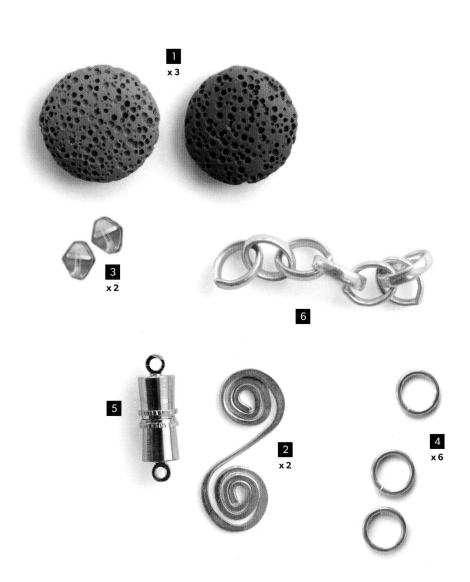

You will need:

1 3 x lava pebbles (more for a larger wrist)

2 12in (30cm) length x US 20 gauge (SWG 21, 0.08mm) silver-plated copper wire to make two spirals

3 2 x 5mm glass beads

4 6 x 8mm jumprings

5 1 x magnetic clasp with jumprings attached

6 Short length of fancy silver chain

39in (1m) length of US 24 gauge (SWG 25, 0.5mm) fine silver wire

Round-nose pliers

Flat-nose pliers

Chain-nose pliers

1 Cut two lengths of US 20 gauge (SWG 21, 0.8mm) wire to a length of 4in (10cm). Make a tiny coil at one end using the point of the round-nose pliers. Grip the coil in the jaws of the flat-nose pliers and make three tight coils. Repeat this action at the other end of the wire to make two coiled links going in the opposite direction.

2 Place a wire coil on a steel block and hammer the coil to flatten it out. Once both ends have been hammered, turn the coil over and flatten the opposite side. Hammer the second coil, then bend the coils slightly in the center so that they curve around your wrist.

3 Cut off a 3¼in (8cm) length of US 24 gauge (SWG 25, 0.5mm) wire and make a wrapped loop at one end. Thread the end of the wire under the coiled link and up through the hole in its center. Next, slide a blue bead onto the wire.

4 Pass the wire back down through the hole in the other coil. Pull the wire tight until the bead sits on the coil link. Make another wrapped loop at the end of the wire. Repeat steps 3 and 4 to decorate the second coiled loop.

5 Cut three 3¼in (8cm) lengths of US 24 gauge (SWG 25, 0.5mm)wire. Then make a wrapped loop at one end of a piece of wire. Pass the free end through one of the lava pebbles and secure it with another wrapped loop. Link the pebble to the coiled link using a 8mm jumpring. Repeat this step for all the pebbles, linking each one to the coils.

6 To finish, cut the chain in half and link it to the magnetic clasp with jumprings. Attach the free ends of the chain to the remaining wrapped loops that extend from the three lava pebbles.

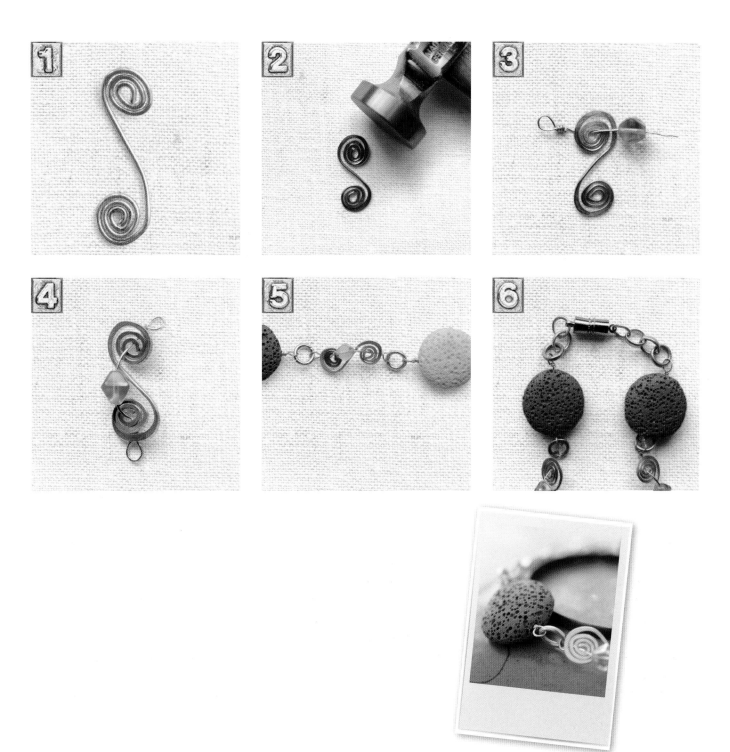

twinkle

Add a dash of sparkle to your look with this delicate, pretty tiara. Get a load of mileage out of a 1950s' sparkly crystal necklace or old pearls by twisting the beads into a dreamy shape that can be worn many different ways.

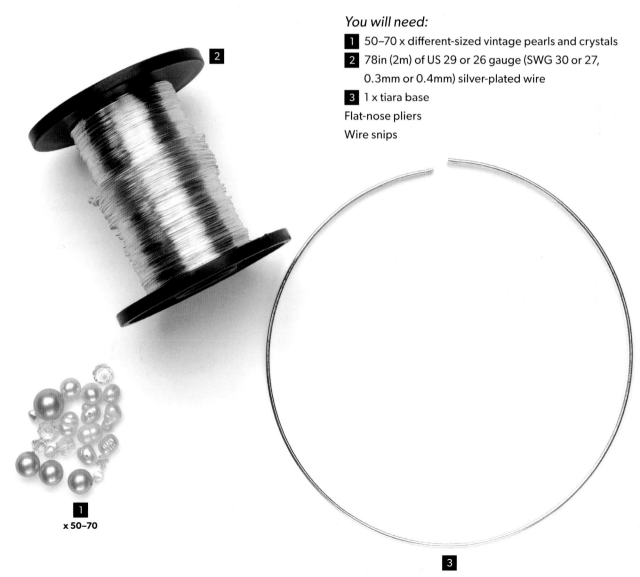

You will need:

1 50–70 x different-sized vintage pearls and crystals
2 78in (2m) of US 29 or 26 gauge (SWG 30 or 27, 0.3mm or 0.4mm) silver-plated wire
3 1 x tiara base
Flat-nose pliers
Wire snips

1
x 50–70

1 If you're using an old necklace, break it up with your pliers. Cut about 12in (30cm) of the wire, thread on your first pearl and push it to the middle point of the wire. Bring both pieces of wire together underneath the bead and then twist the bead with your finger and thumb so that the ends of wire twist together for about 1in (2.5cm).

2 Next, thread a pearl onto one of the ends of wire, fold it at a point about ½in (12mm) from the center trunk and twist the pearl so that the wire forms a branch that joins the main trunk. Do the same with a pearl on the other wire end.

3 Twist the two wire ends together to continue the trunk downward, then take the ends out to each side again. This time add two pearls at separate points on each branch, twisting after each pearl.

4 Continue the trunk down a few twists, then add another branch with two pearls on the other side.

5 Add another pair of branches. Twist the two ends together a bit before making the opposite branch to make it look less regular and more natural. When you're happy with the pearls on your branch, continue twisting the two ends of wire together to create a stalk that you can use to attach it to the tiara.

6 Make five "trees" in this way and vary it as much as you like. You can add two beads at separate points of the branch or add several small beads in one loop at the top, as shown here.

7 Once you've made your trees, lay them out to plan how you'd like them to sit on the tiara. You could aim for quite a traditional shape with the design rising in the middle, or arrange them all at the same height for a more 1950s' retro look.

8 Pull the ends of the tiara base outward to create a horseshoe shape that's more comfortable to wear. Attach the middle branch first by wrapping it at least three times around the middle point of the tiara base, either side of the branch "stem." Work from the middle outward and attach the other branches firmly in the same way. Squeeze any loose ends flat with the pliers (see page 341), and you're done!

Tip *The tiara looks best if you vary the branches and trees. When you've attached all the wire branches, bend and crush them a bit to make them look less regimented.*

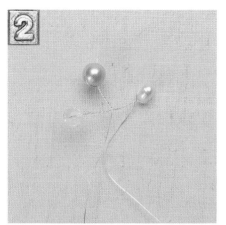

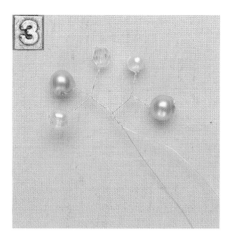

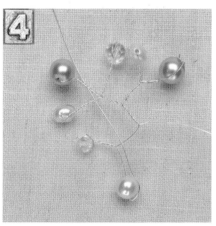

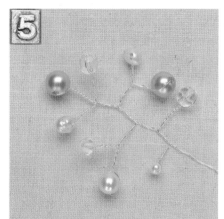

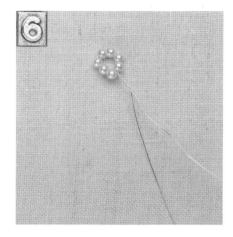

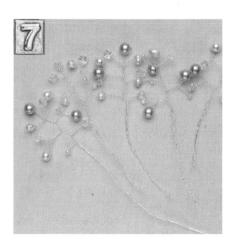

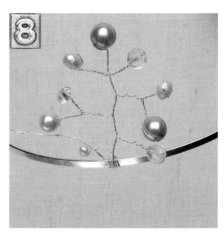

Tip *Wrap soft organza ribbon along the tiara base between and over the wrapped wire for a neat finish and to tone in with your hair.*

peacock

A scanned image of a peacock feather glued into a bezel and topped with a glass dome creates a simple but stylish ring. Use the photo here in the bezel or your own printed picture, collage, Inkjet-printed picture, or piece of fabric.

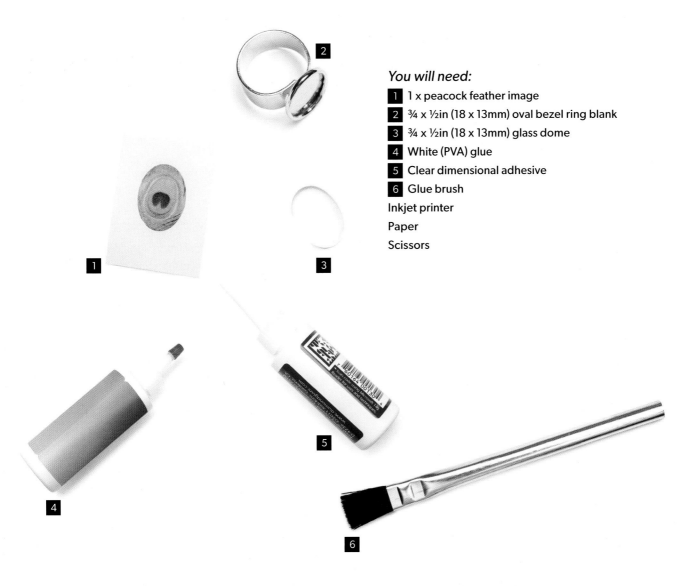

You will need:

1. 1 x peacock feather image
2. ¾ x ½in (18 x 13mm) oval bezel ring blank
3. ¾ x ½in (18 x 13mm) glass dome
4. White (PVA) glue
5. Clear dimensional adhesive
6. Glue brush

Inkjet printer

Paper

Scissors

1 Scan the peacock feather image and print it out, then water down a small amount of white (PVA) glue and paint over the whole image. Allow to dry, then add another two coats. This is to stop the ink from running.

2 Cut the image out so it fits into the ring bezel.

3 Coat the back of the image with clear dimensional adhesive and stick inside the ring bezel. Leave to dry for about 10 minutes.

4 Cover the front of the image with more clear dimensional adhesive.

5 Press the glass dome down firmly on top of the image. Make sure there are no bubbles and then leave to dry thoroughly before wearing.

Tip *Do not shake the clear dimensional adhesive before using as this will create bubbles under the glass.*

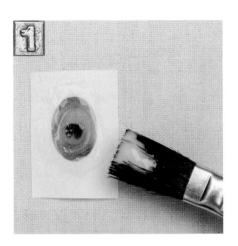

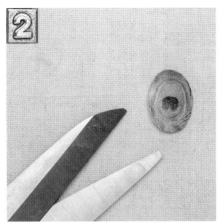

Tip *If you are using a different image from the one provided and need to get the correct size, take your glass dome, place it on the part of the image you like, draw around it, and then cut it out slightly inside the lines.*

felix

Cute and colorful paw prints are ideal adornments for a pair of cufflinks. Polymer clay is a great material for this kind of project as you can bake one part, then add unbaked clay and bake the whole thing again! This keeps the color separation sharp and stops the paw print from going out of shape.

You will need:

1. 1in (25mm) square by ½in (12mm) thick block of blue polymer clay
2. ½in (12mm) ball of pearl white clay
3. 2 x silver-colored cuff links with ⅜in (10mm) pad
4. E6000 glue
5. Polyurethane gloss varnish

¹³/₁₆ x ½in (20 x 12mm) oval cutter

⅜in (10mm) round cutter

⅛in (2mm) round cutter

2in (50mm) square of emery paper

Paintbrush

Teflon sheet

Roller

Spacers or playing cards

Sticky tack

Tip Polymer clay comes in a large variety of colors so pick two that complement each other and suit your outfit.

1 Working on a Teflon sheet, condition the polymer clay by flattening it out with a roller, folding it over and repeating until soft. Then roll it out to about 1⁄16in (1.5mm) thick using the spacers. If you're using playing cards you will need a stack of four each side of the clay. You will need a large enough sheet to cut out four ovals. Using the oval cutter, cut out two ovals but don't remove them from the surrounding clay yet as the clay works to protect the shapes from distorting.

2 With the 3⁄8in (10mm) and 1⁄8in (2mm) round cutters (using the step photo as reference), cut out a paw shape. The 3⁄8in cutter will make the pad of the paw and the 1⁄8in one makes the four toes. Try to stop the clay coming out with the cutter as it's still protecting the shape from distorting.

3 When all the pieces are cut out, gently remove all the cutout pieces to reveal the paw shape.

4 Place the piece from step 3 back on top of the rolled out blue sheet of clay from step 1.

5 Take the oval cutter and, lining it up with the oval shape, press down to cut through the bottom sheet too. As you push down, the two sheets will press together. Bake the pieces following the clay manufacturer's directions.

6 When the baked clay pieces have cooled, fill in the cutout paw shapes with the pearl white clay, pressing the clay into the holes to make sure there are no air holes. Allow the white clay to be slightly higher than the blue and don't worry if it looks a little messy. Bake again to the same temperature.

7 When the clay has cooled again, sand the fronts until the paw outlines look clean and sharp.

8 Sand the cuff link pad and glue the polymer paw prints to the cuff link. Leave to dry.

9 Stand the cuff links up with a little sticky tack and paint the whole polymer piece with a coat of gloss varnish. Leave to dry before wearing.

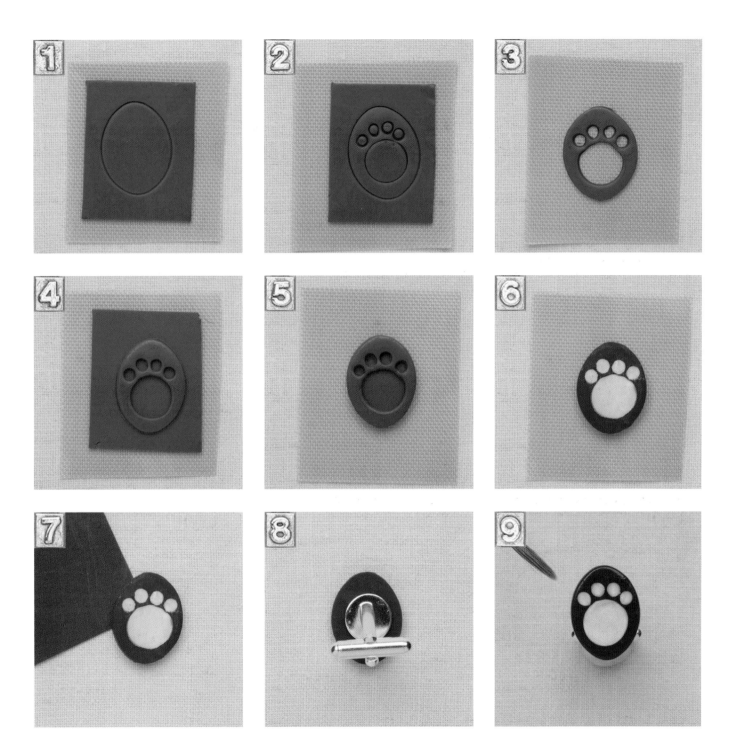

roxy

Rock your world with these fun plectrum earrings. Plectrums are available in different thicknesses, ranging from thin to extra heavy; for these earrings it is best to choose the thin variety.

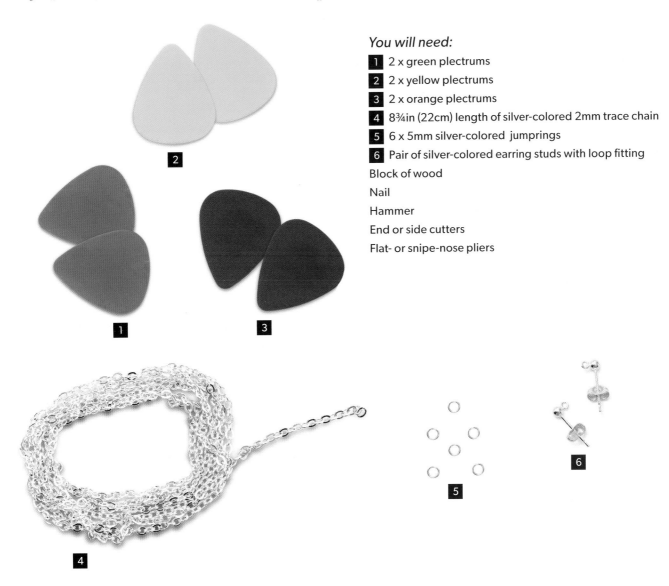

You will need:

1 2 x green plectrums
2 2 x yellow plectrums
3 2 x orange plectrums
4 8¾in (22cm) length of silver-colored 2mm trace chain
5 6 x 5mm silver-colored jumprings
6 Pair of silver-colored earring studs with loop fitting
Block of wood
Nail
Hammer
End or side cutters
Flat- or snipe-nose pliers

1 Ensure you are working on a solid, stable surface such as a block of wood. Place a plectrum on the wood. Position the nail about ⅛in (3mm) from the top of the plectrum in the center. Tap the nail with the hammer approximately three times until the nail has punctured the plectrum and made a small hole. Repeat this stepwith all six plectrums.

2 Cut two pieces of chain to 2⅛in (5.5cm), cut another two pieces to 1⅜in (3.5cm) and cut another two pieces of chain to ¾in (2cm), using the end or side cutters.

3 Using the pliers, open the 5mm jumprings (see page 332) and thread through the holes in the plectrums.

4 Attach a green plectrum to the end of one of the 2⅛in (5.5cm) chains. Attach an orange plectrum to the end of one of the 1⅜in (3.5cm) chains. Attach a yellow plectrum to one of the ¾in (2cm) chains.

5 Take a stud with loop fitting and thread the ¾in (2cm) chain with yellow plectrum onto the loop. Then thread the 1⅜in (3.5cm) chain with orange plectrum onto the loop and finally thread the 2⅛in (5.5cm) chain with green plectrum onto the loop. It is important to put the chains on in this order so that the plectrums hang correctly.

6 Close the loop on the stud with the pliers.

7 Repeat steps 5, 6, and 7 to make a matching earring.

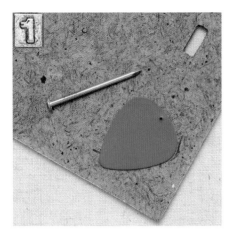

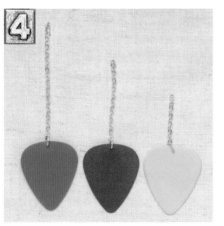

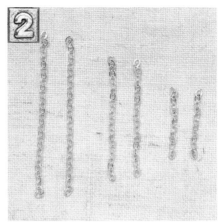

Tip *There are lots of colored and patterned plectrums available, so have fun experimenting with different designs!*

cameo

Take inspiration from the Victorian era and use velvet ribbon to hold a "cameo"—one of the Victorians' favorite pieces of jewelry. Diamante buckles come in a variety of shapes, so you can make your necklace truly unique.

You will need:

1 1 x ½in (12mm) round diamanté buckle
2 14in (35cm) black velvet ribbon, ⅝in (15mm) wide
3 2 x 12mm large ribbon crimps
4 2 x 4mm oval jumprings
5 1 x 7mm jumpring
6 1 x 12mm lobster clasp
7 1 x 2in (50mm) chain extender
8 2 x 2in (50mm) eyepins
9 1 x 20mm cameo bead
10 1 x 10mm black rose bead
11 1 x 4mm diamanté round charm
Flat-nose pliers
Round-nose pliers
Top or side cutters
Scissors

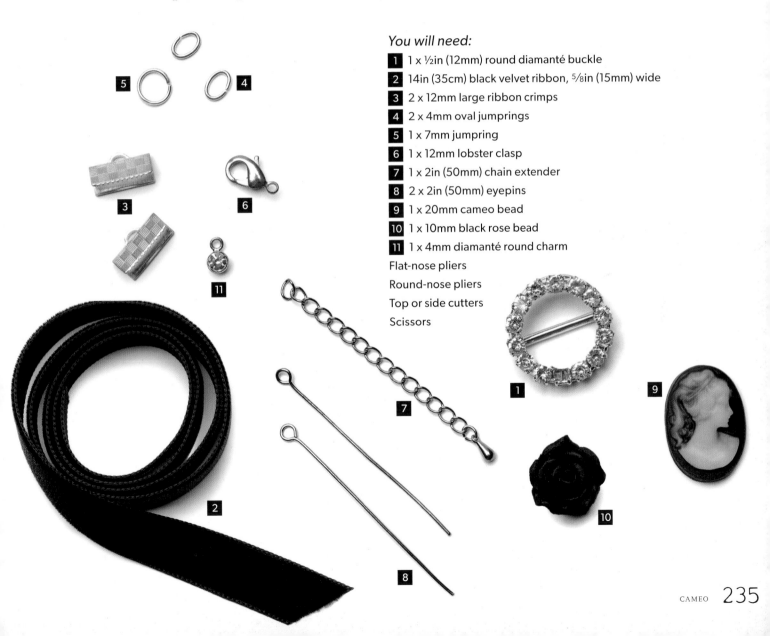

1 Thread the diamanté buckle onto the length of velvet ribbon.

2 Place one end of the velvet ribbon in the jaws of a ribbon crimp. If the ribbon crimp is smaller than the width of your ribbon, just gather the ribbon slightly so that it fits in nicely. There are teeth on the jaws of ribbon crimps, so it's quite easy to hold the ribbon in place. Squash the jaws of the crimp tightly together using flat-nose pliers.

3 Place the ribbon around your neck and mark where you need to place the other ribbon crimp. You may need to cut away excess ribbon at this point. Repeat step 2 to attach the other ribbon crimp to the other end of the velvet. Attach a 4mm oval jumpring and lobster clasp to one end. Attach the other 4mm oval jumpring and a 7mm jumpring holding the chain extender to the other end.

4 Thread an eyepin through your cameo bead and make a large eye loop as close to the top of the cameo as possible. Thread this eye loop through the back of the diamanté buckle and close. Center the diamante buckle on the black velvet ribbon so that the cameo dangles at the front.

5 Thread an eyepin through the rose bead and make an eye loop as close to the top as possible. Link it to the bottom eye loop on the cameo and close. Link the diamanté charm to the bottom eye loop on the rose and close.

Tip *Using a chain extender is a great idea with this style of necklace. It enables you to adjust the length of the choker easily to fit any size of neck.*

claudia

You shall go to the ladybug ball with this fabulous feather and bead fascinator! There are endless possibilities with this design; experiment with different colored feathers for a variety of effects.

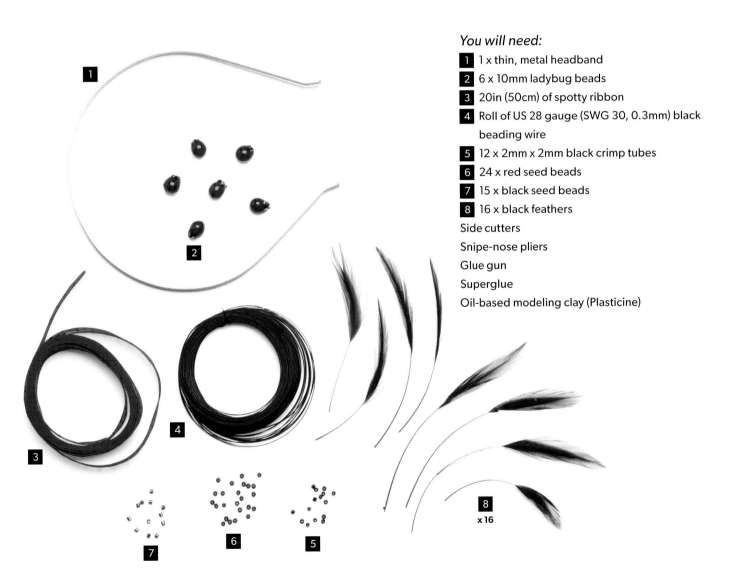

You will need:

1. 1 x thin, metal headband
2. 6 x 10mm ladybug beads
3. 20in (50cm) of spotty ribbon
4. Roll of US 28 gauge (SWG 30, 0.3mm) black beading wire
5. 12 x 2mm x 2mm black crimp tubes
6. 24 x red seed beads
7. 15 x black seed beads
8. 16 x black feathers

Side cutters

Snipe-nose pliers

Glue gun

Superglue

Oil-based modeling clay (Plasticine)

x 16

1 Cut 16in (40cm) of beading wire from the roll and hold it between your fingers at about 7in (18cm) from one end. At this point, start to wrap the wire tightly around the metal headband slightly off-center. After a couple of coils make sure the other long end of wire, now also approximately 7in (18cm) long, is coming off the opposite side of the headband from where you started.

2 Cut another two 16in (40cm) lengths of wire and wrap them in the same way so you have a group of six wires coiled around the hair band in one spot. Plug in your glue gun and allow it to heat up.

3 Take the black feathers and cut them so they are at least 4in (10cm) in length. Hold the feather by the quill and gently pinch it between your thumbnail and forefinger. The pulling action is much like curling gift ribbon and will make the quill have a good curve. You can add a few seed beads to some of the quills using a drop of superglue at each bead.

4 Stand the metal headband in a lump of soft modeling clay (Plasticine) so it is secure and the group of wires that you wrapped on earlier are facing the top and are accessible to work on. Carefully add a tiny drop of melted

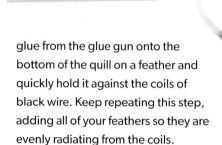

glue from the glue gun onto the bottom of the quill on a feather and quickly hold it against the coils of black wire. Keep repeating this step, adding all of your feathers so they are evenly radiating from the coils.

5 Working on one wire at a time, cut each length so they are all about 6in (15cm) long. Again, hold the wire between your thumbnail and forefinger and curl it. Add a tiny drop of superglue along the wire and add a red seed bead. Add three seed beads per wire, leaving at least 1½in (4cm) clear from each end.

6 Take a black crimp tube and squash it flat on the wire using snipe-nose pliers approximately 1¼in (3cm) from the end of the wire. Add a ladybug bead and then another crimp tube. Again, squash the crimp tube flat as close to the top of the ladybug bead as possible, trapping it in place on the wire. Repeat this step to add ladybugs to all the wires.

7 Add another drop of superglue to the end tip of the wire and glue a red seed bead right at the end. Repeat this step, adding red seed beads to the ends of all of the wires.

8 Cut 8in (20cm) of beading wire and at the center point, tie a double bow onto it using your spotty ribbon. The overall size of the bow can be as large as you like. Cut the ends of the bow so you have pointed tails.

9 Hold the bow as firmly as possible against all of the wires and feathers to conceal the glue and wire where it all joins to the headband. Neatly coil the long ends of wire that run through the bow around the metal band at either end. Cut away any excess wire.

julia

Make a delightfully handmade statement with this felt flower brooch.
Fabulously cute and finished off with a pretty pearl button, it is easy
to sew and sure to raise a smile.

You will need:
1   4 x 8in (10 x 20cm) of thin felt
2   1 x pearl button
3   1 x brooch pin
4   Thread to match the felt
Needle
Scissors

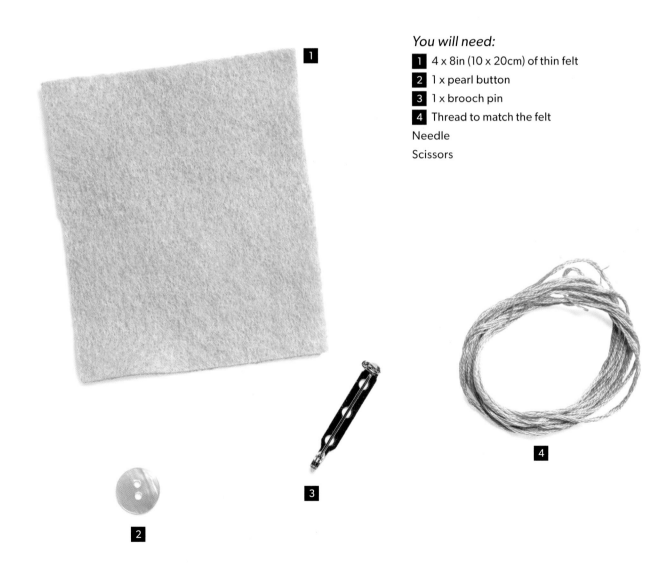

1 Cut out three flowers in felt using the templates below as guides.

2 Take the largest one and fold it in half with the opposing petals aligned. Sew a tight blanket stitch (see page 346) along the folded ridge, leaving ⅝in (1.5cm) open at both ends. Secure with a few small stitches.

3 Now re-fold the flower with two more opposing flower petals aligned. As you fold across the already stitched ridge it will get a little hard to sew —just stitch through the center. Re-fold for a third time and you

should have a finished result that looks like the step image. Sew all three flower pieces in the same way.

4 Layer all three flowers together, aligning the largest and smallest ones and placing the middle one with the petals in between the other two.

5 From the back, sew through all the layers, securing them together. Sew through a few times without the button in the center, then position the button and sew through it a few times to secure.

6 Place the brooch pin on one of the sewn ridges at the back and sew on using the three holes in the brooch bar. Make sure it is well secured before knotting off the thread.

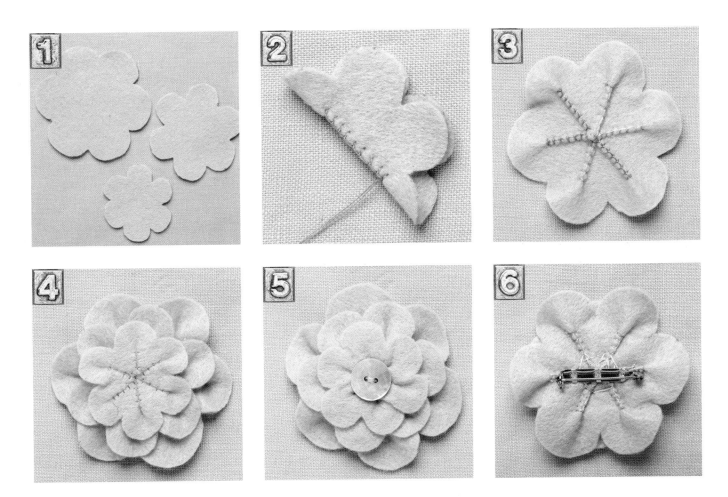

Tip *This flower would look brilliant sewn onto a headband or attached to a hair grip.*

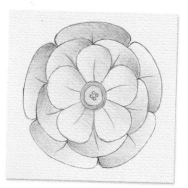

daisy

Cheerful and charming as a daisy itself! Use knotted black twine interlaced with hand-painted wooden beads to create a very simple piece that can be made anywhere and in no time at all.

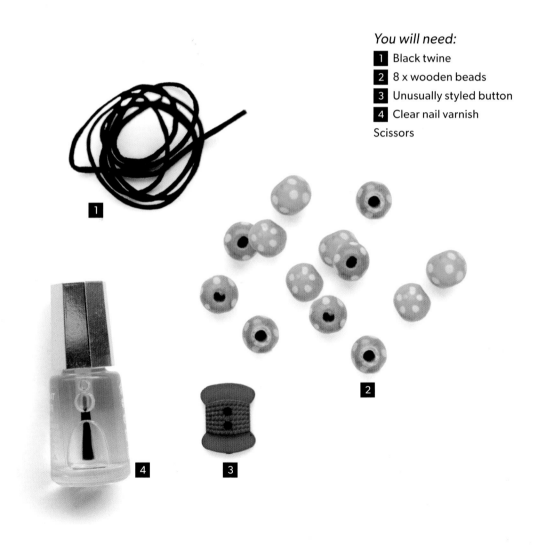

You will need:
1 Black twine
2 8 x wooden beads
3 Unusually styled button
4 Clear nail varnish
Scissors

1 Cut approximately 39in (1m) of twine. Fold it in half and hold the fold in the fingers of your dominant hand. Tie a simple knot in the twine, leaving a loop at the end to act as a fastener.

2 Separate the two ends of twine and lay them flat. Pass one end through the center of a wooden bead. Then pass the second strand through the other side of the hole, bringing it out on the opposite side of the bead from where it entered the hole.

3 Thread another bead onto the twine, passing the yarn through the center of the bead so that it crosses over. Slide this bead towards the first bead to create approximately a 1in (2.5cm) space between the two beads.

4 Continue to weave the beads onto the two strands of twine. Check the length of the twine against your wrist for the correct size. When you have reached this length, tie the two strands of twine together in a neat knot.

5 Attach a clasp onto the end of the bracelet that doesn't have a loop. Pass the ends of the twine through the holes of an unusually shaped button and tie them into a knot.

6 Cut the ends of the twine so that they are neat and tidy. Finish by dabbing a little nail varnish onto the cut ends to prevent them from fraying.

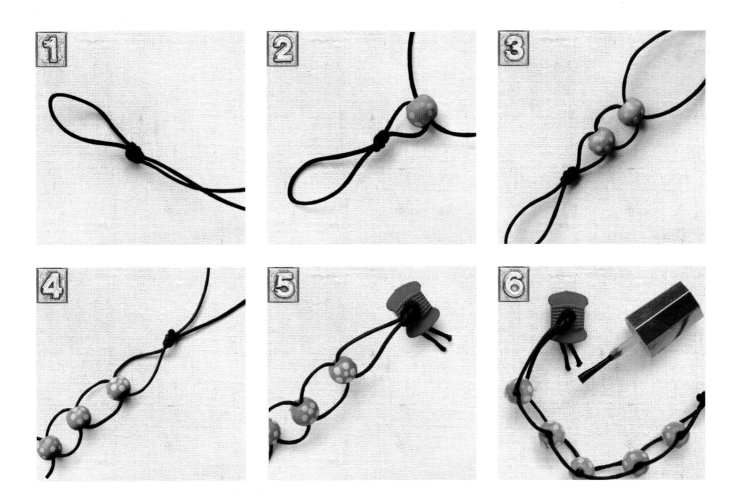

Tip *Instead of reading a book to pass the time, pull out a roll of twine and knot up some bright cheerful bracelets.*

florence

These bird chandelier fittings sparked the idea for a pair of pretty garden-themed earrings with a Victorian touch. Keeping the colors muted and using real freshwater pearls add to the old-fashioned feel.

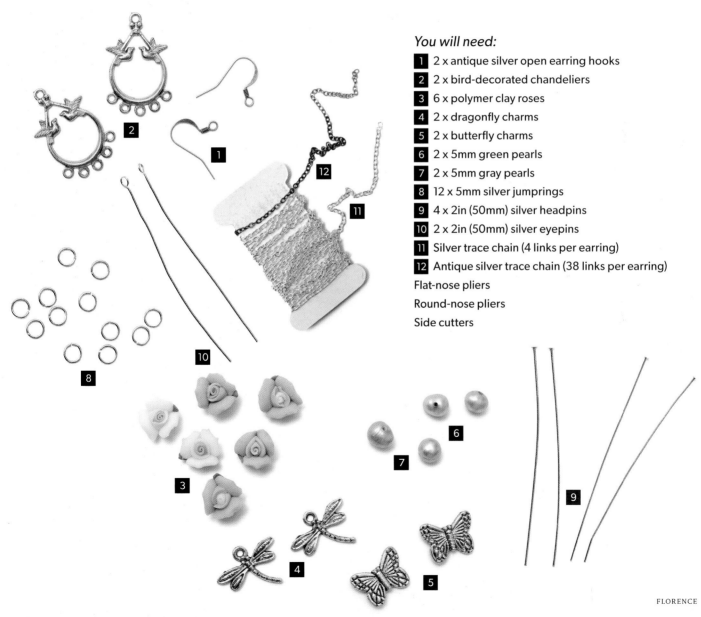

You will need:

1. 2 x antique silver open earring hooks
2. 2 x bird-decorated chandeliers
3. 6 x polymer clay roses
4. 2 x dragonfly charms
5. 2 x butterfly charms
6. 2 x 5mm green pearls
7. 2 x 5mm gray pearls
8. 12 x 5mm silver jumprings
9. 4 x 2in (50mm) silver headpins
10. 2 x 2in (50mm) silver eyepins
11. Silver trace chain (4 links per earring)
12. Antique silver trace chain (38 links per earring)

Flat-nose pliers

Round-nose pliers

Side cutters

1 Insert a 2in (5cm) headpin into a polymer clay rose and wrap the long end of the wire around the bottom of the chandelier fitting. Repeat this step using the two other flowers.

2 Open a 5mm jumpring (see page 332) and thread it onto the antique silver chain (38 links long). Link it onto the left hoop on the chandelier fitting, then close. Take another jumpring and link this onto the bottom end of the chain and to the far right loop on the chandelier fitting.

3 Open a third jumpring, thread it through a dragonfly charm and the next loop on the chandelier fitting, then close.

4 Thread a 2in (50mm) headpin through a butterfly charm. Make an eye loop as close to the top of the butterfly as possible, then cut off any excess wire.

5 Open and thread another jumpring onto a length of silver chain (4 links long), link this to the top of the butterfly eye loop, then close. Link another open jumpring to the top of the small chain and to the middle loop on the chandelier fitting, then close.

6 Thread a 2in (50mm) headpin through a green pearl. Make an eye loop as close to the top of the pearl as possible.

7 Thread a 2in (50mm) eyepin through a gray pearl, and make an eye loop as close to the pearl as possible. Use this to link the green pearl, then close.

8 Open a final jumpring and thread it through the top eye loop of the gray pearl and the last remaining loop on the chandelier fitting.

9 Open the loop on an earring hook, link this to the chandelier fitting and close. Repeat the process to create the other earring.

Tip *If desired, create the second earring as a mirror image. You will need to change the bead order to achieve this.*

streamlined

This stunning hair accessory captures the style and elegance displayed by many of our feathered friends and is very simple to make. This project uses feathers ready bound with tiny decorative feathers at the base. The ends are neatly finished in black tape.

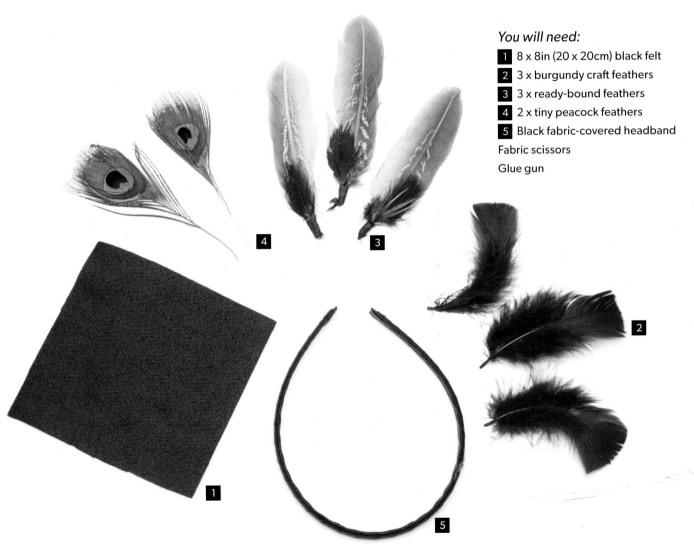

You will need:

1 8 x 8in (20 x 20cm) black felt
2 3 x burgundy craft feathers
3 3 x ready-bound feathers
4 2 x tiny peacock feathers
5 Black fabric-covered headband
Fabric scissors
Glue gun

1 Cut two identical teardrop shapes out of the black felt, approximately 5in (13cm) long by 3in (7.5cm) at the widest point.

2 Position your three burgundy feathers at the top of the felt, in a fan shape, with the middle feather slightly higher than the other two. Make sure you can't see any of the felt at the top or sides of the feathers.

3 Put a line of hot glue onto the felt underneath each feather. Press and hold each feather for a few minutes to ensure it is secure.

4 Cover the remaining felt in a good amount of hot glue and place your three ready bound feathers, again in a fan shape, onto the glue and press and hold. Also put a tiny blob underneath the top of each feather and press down to secure to the feathers underneath.

5 Cut two small peacock feathers to about 3in (7.5cm). Put a small blob of hot glue on the end of each one and slide down behind the tiny feathers at the base of the thinner feathers. Also put a blob of hot glue on the feather underneath the top of each peacock feather and press and hold.

6 Squeeze a thick line of hot glue all the way along the underside of your feather decoration.

7 Place the decoration onto the headband approximately 2–2½in (5–6cm) from the end, so the glue runs along it. Press down hard and hold both ends down until the glue sets. Don't worry if the glue spills out onto the felt.

8 Cover the second piece of felt with hot glue but not quite to the edges as you don't want it to ooze out of the sides.

9 Match up to the felt on the back of your decoration, place down and gently press, and hold until the glue has dried.

Tip *If the base of your feather decoration looks untidy with lots of feather ends showing, find a pretty button large enough to cover it and simply hot glue it on top.*

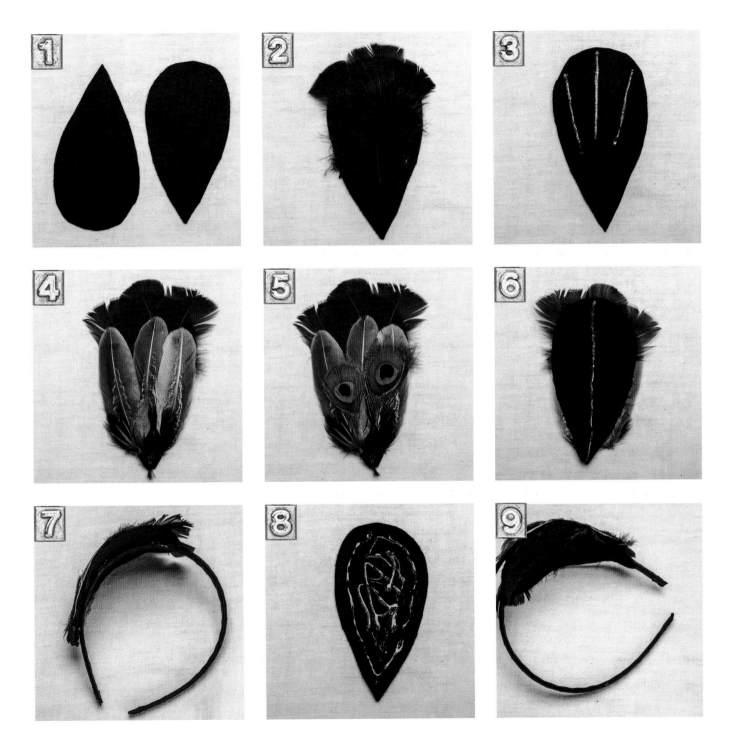

luna

This pretty patterned cat button makes a colorful ring. Decoupage is a great way to decorate anything, so lovely cat button shapes like these just shout out to be patterned.

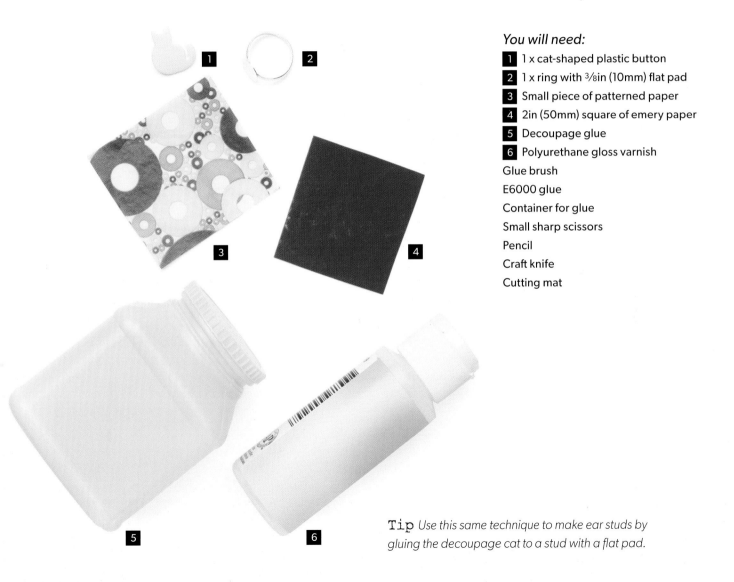

You will need:

1 1 x cat-shaped plastic button
2 1 x ring with ⅜in (10mm) flat pad
3 Small piece of patterned paper
4 2in (50mm) square of emery paper
5 Decoupage glue
6 Polyurethane gloss varnish
Glue brush
E6000 glue
Container for glue
Small sharp scissors
Pencil
Craft knife
Cutting mat

Tip *Use this same technique to make ear studs by gluing the decoupage cat to a stud with a flat pad.*

1 Take the button and sand the front to provide a key for the decoupage.

2 With the patterned paper and a pencil, draw an outline of the cat button on the back of the paper. Take your time to work out which part of the paper pattern you want on the cat.

3 Cut out the cat shape leaving ⅛in (3mm) around the outside of the pencil line. After cutting the shape out, go around the edge and make small cuts up to the pencil line to make the edge into lots of little tabs. This helps the paper bend around the shape when you glue it on.

Tip If the button is made of soft plastic, you can cut off the shank with an old pair of side cutters. Don't use a new pair as it could blunt them.

4 Pour a small amount of decoupage glue into a container and paint a layer of glue on the front of the cat button. Holding the button by the shank on the back, carefully place the paper on the cat, lining up the pencil outline to the edge of the cat. Paint a layer of glue over the top of the paper.

5 With a tiny amount of glue on your brush, go around the edge and paste each tab down the sides. Work slowly and make sure you take off any spare glue with the brush as you go. Leave the button to dry completely.

6 Take the craft knife and carefully cut the shank off the back of the button. As it's plastic it should be fairly easy to cut off, but this should only be done by an adult.

7 Take the ring blank and sand the flat pad, then place a small amount of glue on the pad and stick the cat button down. Leave to completely dry before wearing.

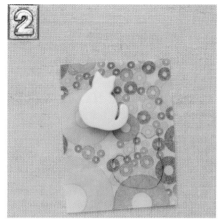

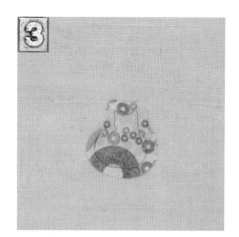

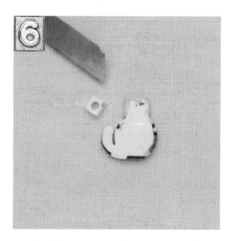

Tip *This design works with buttons that have holes too, just follow the steps but skip step 6. The paper will cover the holes and the glue will fill them when attached to the ring blank.*

audrey

Film star Audrey Hepburn's iconic outfits teamed pearls with a little black dress. Here's how to make your own version of a classic look! Joining beads to make actual links gives an unusual twist to simple stringing.

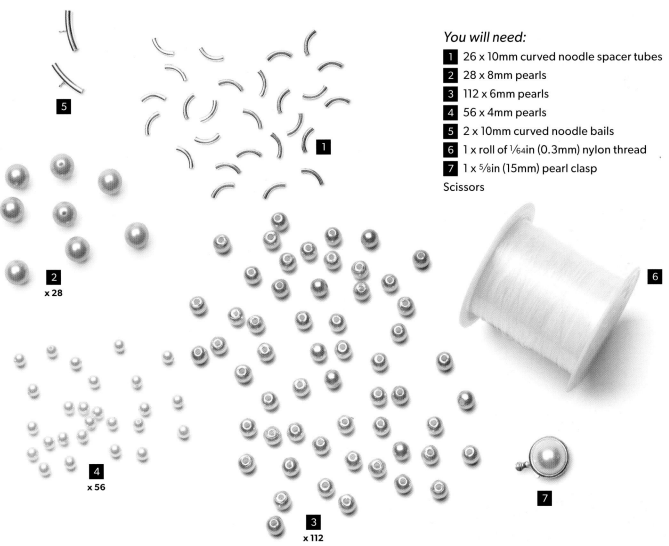

You will need:

1. 26 x 10mm curved noodle spacer tubes
2. 28 x 8mm pearls
3. 112 x 6mm pearls
4. 56 x 4mm pearls
5. 2 x 10mm curved noodle bails
6. 1 x roll of ¹⁄₆₄in (0.3mm) nylon thread
7. 1 x ⁵⁄₈in (15mm) pearl clasp

Scissors

1 Place 2 x curved noodle spacer tubes, 2 x 8mm pearls, 8 x 6mm pearls and 4 x 4mm pearls on a bead mat, laid out as shown in the photo.

2 Cut a 12-in (30cm) length of nylon thread from the roll and thread on all the beads in the order shown in step 1.

3 When all the beads are on, thread one end of the nylon back through all the beads so that it comes round to meet the other end again.

4 Tie a double knot, pulling all the beads together tightly. The noodle spacers at either end will give the overall piece an oval shape. Then thread the ends of the nylon thread back through a couple of the beads and cut off any excess. This prevents you from cutting the nylon too close to the original knot.

Tip Look out for vintage clasps on pieces of old jewelry from charity shops to give your necklace a unique feel.

5 Cut another 12in (30cm) length of nylon and thread on the same formation of beads as in step 1. Then pass one end of the nylon through the first "beaded link" that you completed in step 4.

6 Pass one end of the nylon back through all the beads to meet the other end; you have now joined two "links" together. Repeat step 4 to tie the knot and secure. Repeat steps 5 and 6 until you have made 12 joined beaded links.

7 You now need to make the final two links to add to either end of the necklace. Repeat steps 5 and 6, replacing one noodle spacer tube in each "link" with a noodle bail.

8 Attach a pearl clasp to the noodle bail at each end of the necklace and close.

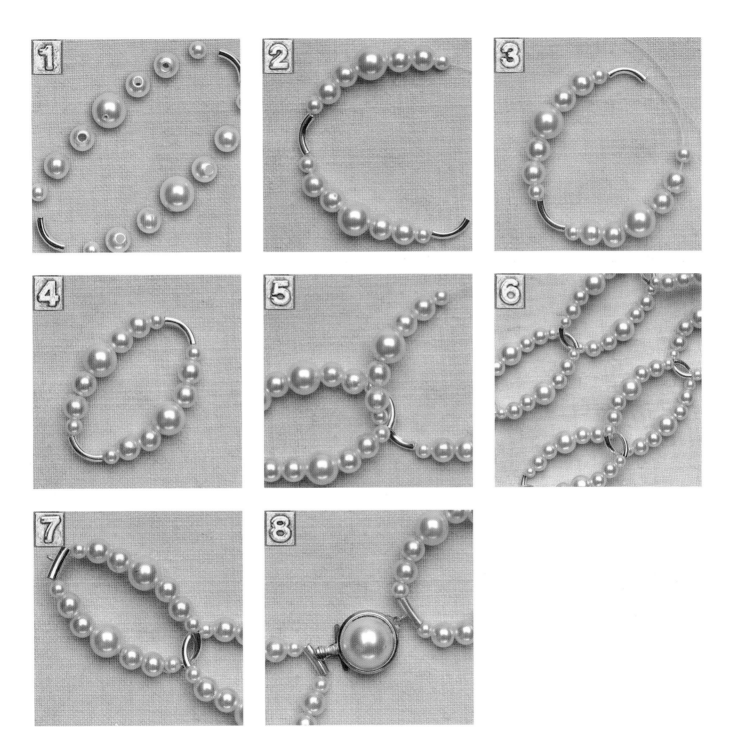

katie

This blooming marvelous hair slide is sure to brighten your day. Shrink plastic is a great material to experiment with. The possibilities are endless and it works really well for both children's and adults' accessories.

You will need:

1 10½ x 8in (26 x 20cm) sheet of frosted shrink plastic

2 2¾ in (7cm) clear comb

3 Pencil

4 Colored pencils in bright yellow, bright pink, white, orange, bright green, and dark green

E6000 glue

Scissors

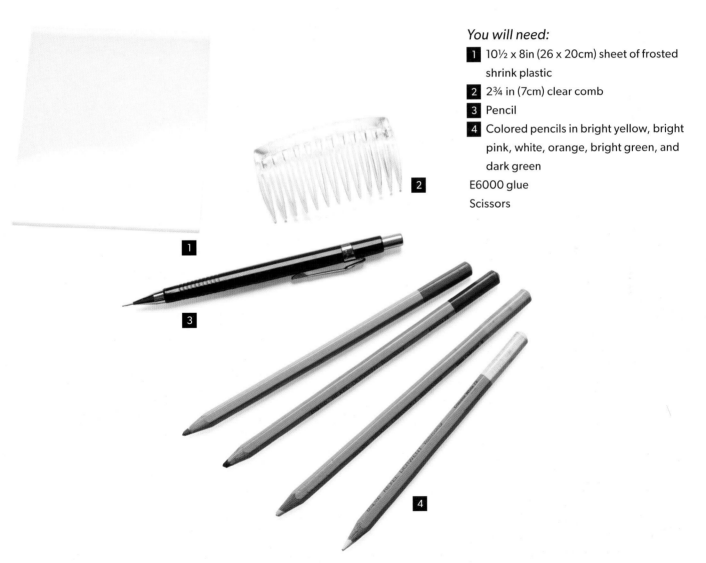

1 Using the template provided, draw the flower shape on the matt side of the shrink plastic. You will be able to see through the frosted plastic so place it on top of the template and trace the outline. Use the yellow pencil to draw the circle in the center and the white pencil to draw the petals. Draw three. Use the bright green pencil to draw three leaf shapes.

2 Cut roughly around each shape. Using the template to see where each color goes, start with the center of the flowers and color them in with bright yellow and then shade half the circle with orange.

3 Color in the petals with white (this will be easier if you place the plastic over a darker color so you can see the white pencil line). Then, using a pink pencil, draw lines out from the center circle. With the longest line in the center of each petal, make shorter lines out toward the edges of the petals.

4 Color in the leaves with bright green. Then go over the edges with darker green and draw in lines from the center. Use the photograph as a guide.

5 Cut out all the pieces. Be careful, as shrink plastic can tear easily. Shrink in a domestic oven using the manufacturer's instructions. Always watch the plastic as it shrinks really quickly and can melt if left in the oven for too long (see page 350). As you take the pieces out of the oven, before they completely cool, lay the flowers face down over a dome shape, such as a light bulb. This is optional as the flowers would look fine flat as well.

6 Let all the pieces cool. Then, using the E6000 glue, stick the three flowers in a line across the top of the comb. Place them so the petals overlap, then glue the leaves in behind the flowers.

Tip *Shrink plastic comes in packs with different flowers already printed on that just need coloring in. This would work well if you are making this project with a child.*

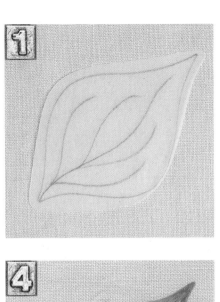

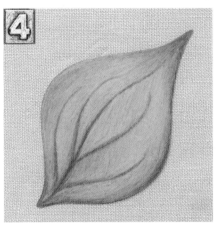

paddy

These tiny paw prints are as cute as a kitten! The little stud earrings are about ³/₈in (10mm), which makes them perfect to wear all day, every day! And all you need to make them is a tiny scrap of clay.

You will need:

1 Metallic copper polymer clay
2 2 x ¼in (6mm) flat pad posts (with scroll backs)
3 Craft knife
4 2 x 2in (50mm) squares of Teflon sheet
5 E6000 glue
2 x chain-nose pliers

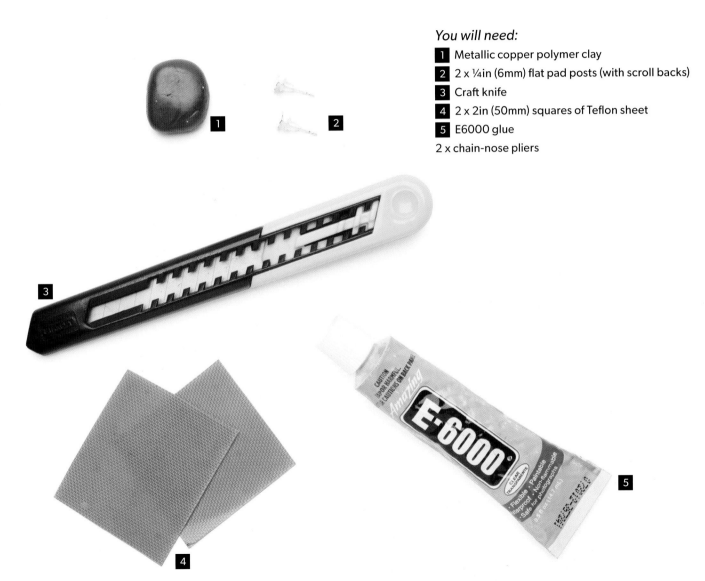

1 Take a pea-size piece of clay and roll it into a log shape about ⅛in (2mm) wide.

2 With the craft knife cut eight equal-size pieces from the roll about ¹⁄₁₆in (1.5mm) long. The exact size doesn't matter too much so long as all the pieces are about the same size.

3 Take another piece of clay and make two identical balls about ³⁄₁₆in (5mm) big. Roll them, individually, into balls. Also roll the tiny slivers from step 2 into balls.

4 Place the larger ball on a piece of Teflon sheet and arrange four of the smaller balls in a line on one side; it should look like a paw at this point. Repeat with the other larger ball and the remaining four smaller balls on the other piece of Teflon sheet. This stage is done on the Teflon so you can transfer the paws into the oven without needing to pick them up as they are very delicate.

5 Make sure your Teflon sheets with the paws in place are on a firm surface, then press gently on the paws with your forefinger. Use a firm pressure so that all the balls squash together and stick. Don't wiggle your finger around, just press straight down.

6 Bake the paw shapes in a toaster oven or a standard oven at the temperature recommended by the clay manufacturer (this will differ depending on the brand of clay you have). Once baked, let the paws cool, and then they will come straight off the sheet. Using a tiny dot of E6000 glue, attach the ear stud pads to the backs of the paws.

Tip *Sometimes the paws come apart after firing, so it's a good idea to make more than two at the same time, then you are guaranteed to have at least two that match and have stuck together.*

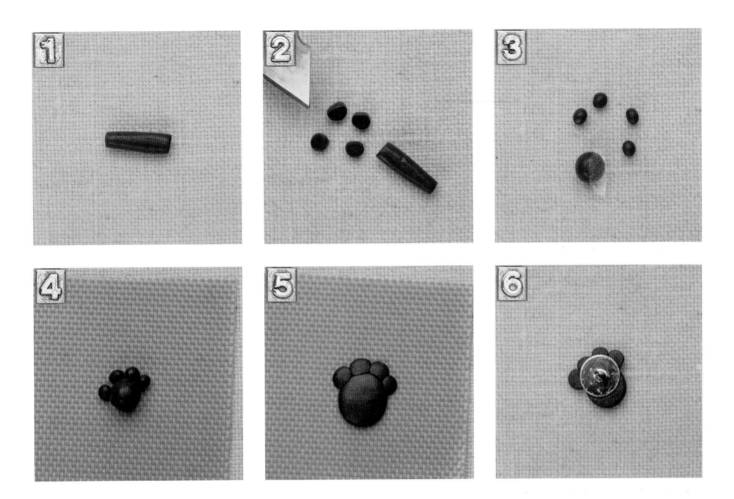

Tip *You can make these paws at whatever size you wish, but as you go bigger you will need something flat to press them with as your finger won't be large enough.*

crystal

Wear your heart on your sleeve and show a loved one that they hold the key to your heart. Sparkle and shine in style by using diamante and crystal charms in your designs.

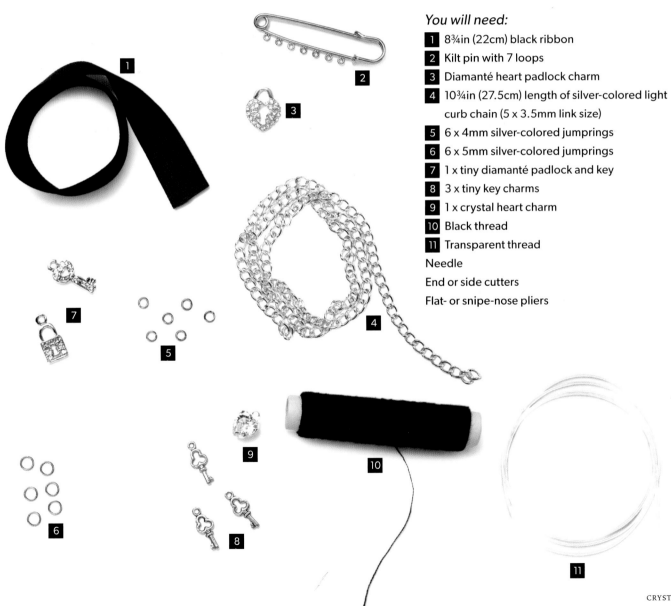

You will need:

1. 8¾in (22cm) black ribbon
2. Kilt pin with 7 loops
3. Diamanté heart padlock charm
4. 10¾in (27.5cm) length of silver-colored light curb chain (5 x 3.5mm link size)
5. 6 x 4mm silver-colored jumprings
6. 6 x 5mm silver-colored jumprings
7. 1 x tiny diamanté padlock and key
8. 3 x tiny key charms
9. 1 x crystal heart charm
10. Black thread
11. Transparent thread

Needle

End or side cutters

Flat- or snipe-nose pliers

1 Make a bow (see page 349). Place the bow over the large loop in the kilt pin at the opposite end to the opening.

2 Place the diamanté padlock over the front center of the bow and, using transparent thread, sew from the back of the bow through the kilt-pin loop and through the middle of the padlock.

3 Loop over the top of the padlock and around the back, coming back through the loop, and repeat until the charm and bow are securely attached to the kilt pin.

4 Repeat the sewing from step 3 but this time loop the thread around the bottom of the padlock and bottom of the loop. When secure, stitch through the ribbon and tie a knot to secure the thread and trim the excess.

5 Using the end or side cutters, cut a piece of chain to 4¼in (11cm), another piece to 2½in (6.5cm), another piece to 2⅜in (6cm), and the last piece to 1½in (4cm).

6 Attach two of the 5mm jumprings to each end of the 4¼in (11cm) chain (see page 332) and then attach one end to the first loop and one end to the last loop on the kilt pin. Then, again using 5mm jumprings, attach one end of the 2½in (6.5cm) chain to the second loop from the left on the kilt pin and one end to the last loop on the right.

7 Use a 5mm jumpring to attach one end of the 2⅜in (6cm) chain to the first loop on the left. Then use a 5mm jumpring to attach one end of the 1½in (4cm) chain to the jumpring at the top of the 2⅜in (6cm) chain.

8 Use 4mm jumprings to attach the diamanté key to the loose end of the 2⅜in (6cm) chain, and the diamanté padlock to the loose end of the 1½in (4cm) chain.

9 Use 3 x 4mm jumprings to attach tiny keys to the sixth, eleventh, and sixteenth links, counting from the top right side, of the longer looped chain. Use the remaining 4mm jumpring to attach the crystal heart to the tenth link, counting from the top left side, of the shorter looped chain.

Tip *To vary the design, use a kilt pin with fewer loops attached along the bottom.*

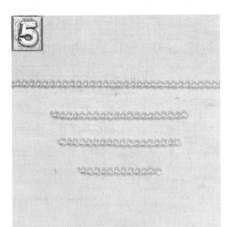

twists

The silver twisted tube spacer beads create a real sense of movement in this simple design. Using multistrand elastic is a great way of stringing beads together without having to use any findings, and it doesn't matter how big or small you make the necklace, as you will be able to stretch it over your head!

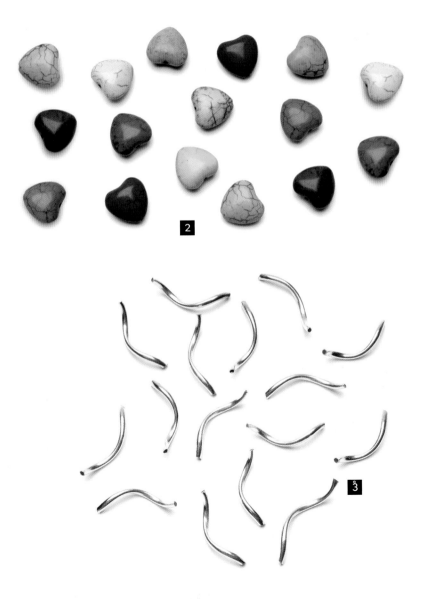

You will need:

1 39in (1m) multistrand elastic
2 16 x 18mm colored heart-shape beads
3 16 x 25mm twisted tube spacer beads
Scissors
Beading needle

1 Arrange the colored heart-shape beads, making sure that no two of the same color are next to each other.

2 Thread your length of multistrand elastic through the eye of the beading needle.

3 Thread on the first colored heart-shape bead, followed by a twisted tube spacer bead.

4 Repeat step 3, but this time thread the heart bead on upside down. Keep alternating heart beads and twisted tube spacer beads, and also the way the heart beads face, until you have used up all the beads.

5 Tie the two ends of the elastic in a knot, pulling the elastic tightly so that all the beads sit flush against each other.

6 Keeping the beading needle on one end of the elastic, thread it back through a few of the beads, so that the end is no longer near the tied knot. Cut off any excess. Thread the beading needle onto the other end of the elastic and repeat this process, going the other way around the necklace.

Tip *If you are using heavier beads such as ceramic or metal, try to keep the necklace short so that the elastic doesn't stretch under the weight.*

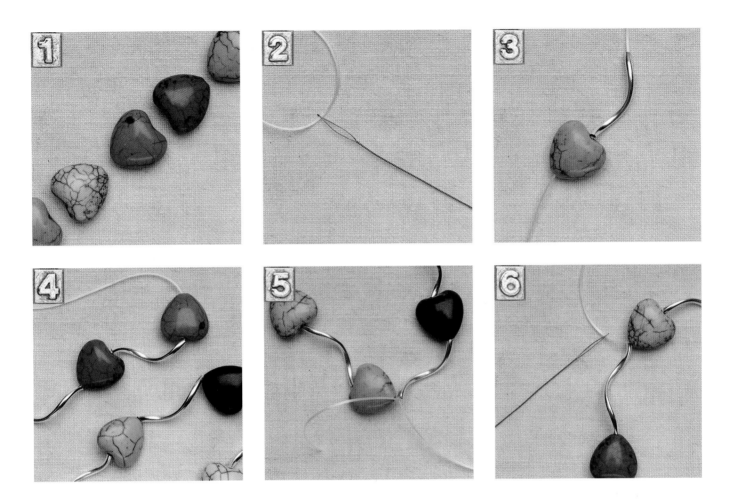

Tip *Stringing beads upright and then upside down, like the heart beads in this project, means there is no right or wrong way to the necklace. It doesn't matter which way round it is worn.*

jem

Stylish and colorful, these resin cufflinks are tailored to please. The subtle floral design will brighten the wrists of any sharp dresser. They are simple, quick, and fun to make.

You will need:

1 Pair of cufflink deep bezel blanks
2 Deep pink and clear resin
3 Resin hardener
4 2 x flower shapes
5 Scraps of polymer clay
Mixing cups and sticks
Jewelers' scales (optional)

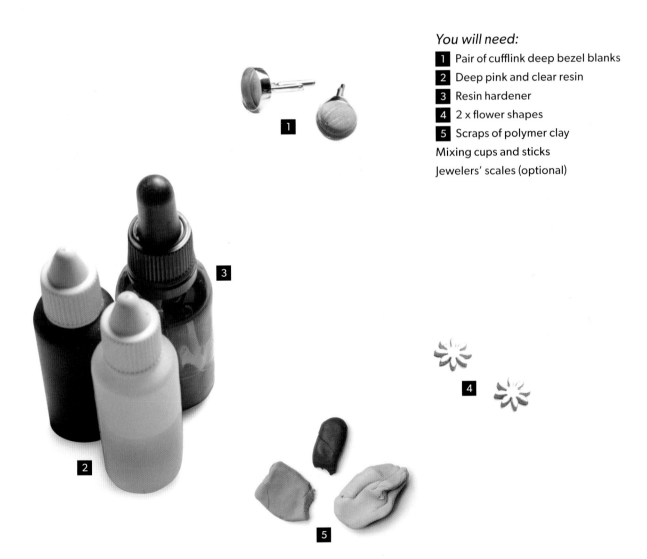

1 Prop both the cufflink blanks up with polymer clay. Make sure the tops are completely horizontal or the resin will not set level.

2 Mix up about $\frac{1}{32}$oz (0.9g) of dark pink resin in a plastic cup. The ratio should be 2:1, resin to hardener. Count out 14 drops of resin and seven drops of hardener from the bottles. For extra accuracy you could use a plastic pipette or jewelers' scales.

3 Mix gently with a wooden stick to make sure no bubbles appear.

4 Place the flower shapes in the bottom of the cufflinks and pour pink resin over the top to the level of the flower, so the flower is sitting in pink resin but you can still see it clearly.

5 Cover the cufflinks with a cup to stop dust from settling in the resin and leave for 24 hours to dry completely.

6 Mix $\frac{1}{64}$oz (0.6g) of clear resin by counting out 10 drops of resin and 5 drops of hardener. Pour it over the pink up to the level of the bezel. Cover with a plastic cup and leave to dry again.

Tip *Instead of using resin why not decorate these blanks with two-part epoxy resin clay and crystals?*

Tip *If bubbles appear in the resin, gently wave a lighter or lit match across the top. The heat will make the bubbles rise and burst. This should only be done when the resin is wet and only by an adult.*

songbird

Take inspiration from the huge trend for decorative birdcages, and create these enchanting miniatures to be worn as earrings. Use feather charms for this project or you could use two different bird charms.

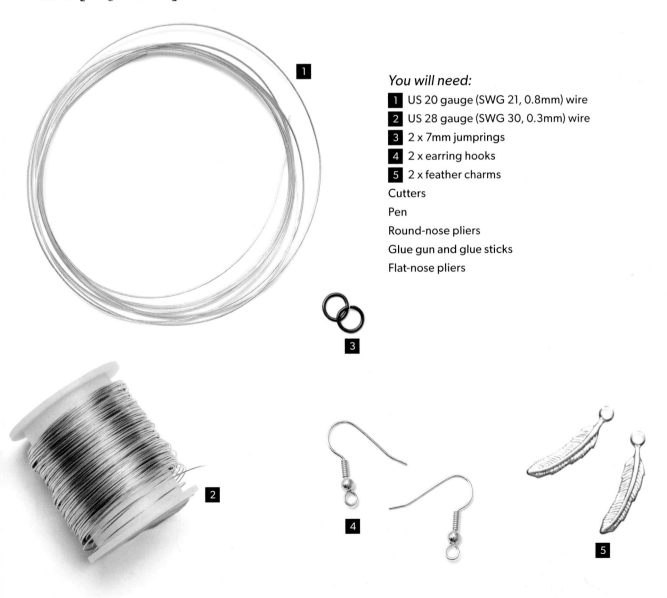

You will need:

1 US 20 gauge (SWG 21, 0.8mm) wire
2 US 28 gauge (SWG 30, 0.3mm) wire
3 2 x 7mm jumprings
4 2 x earring hooks
5 2 x feather charms
Cutters
Pen
Round-nose pliers
Glue gun and glue sticks
Flat-nose pliers

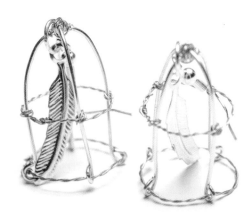

1 Using the cutters, cut four pieces of US 20 gauge (SWG 21, 0.8mm) wire to 3in (7.5cm) long. Bend each wire in half over a pen to form an arch shape. Then, using round-nose pliers, grip the very ends of the wire with the tips of the pliers and turn 180 degrees to form a tiny closed loop on each end.

2 Place one arch on top of the other to form a cross. Lift the top arch away and put a blob of hot glue on the center of the arch below. Replace the top arch and press together. Repeat with the other two arches.

3 Use your fingers to wrap some US 28 gauge (SWG 30, 0.3mm) wire around the glued joint of the arches and pull the end of the wire tightly with the pliers to fully secure the structure.

4 Using the cutters, cut four pieces of US 28 gauge (SWG 30, 0.3mm) to 3in (7.5cm) long. Twist two pieces together tightly and then form into a circle shape, but don't secure the ends. Repeat with the other two pieces of wire.

5 Thread the twisted wire circle through all four of the loops at the ends of the wire arches of one birdcage. Now secure the ends of the wire circle by twisting them around each other twice. Repeat with the second birdcage.

6 Repeat step 4 but cut the wire to 2½in (6cm) and secure the ends of the circles this time. Then slide them over the top of the wire arches until they reach halfway down.

7 Wrap US 28 gauge (SWG 30, 0.3mm) wire around each of the four points that the circle crosses the arches, to secure the whole cage. Do this on both cages.

8 Open a 7mm jumpring widely (see page 332) and thread through the loop of the earring hook. Next, thread on the feather charm and then thread through the top of the birdcage directly across the join at the top. Close the jumpring so the earring is complete. Repeat this on the second birdcage.

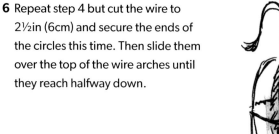

Tip *For a design twist, hang two different charms inside the cages—for example, a gold star in one and a heart in the other.*

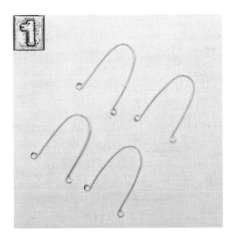

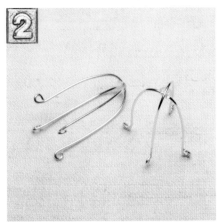

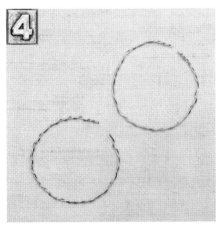

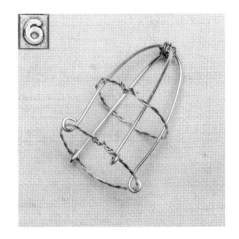

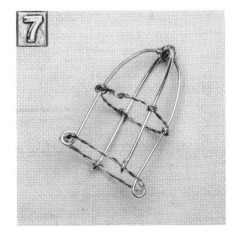

Tip *To achieve secure wire joints and a neat cage, use pliers in each hand to grip the wire and pull it tight when wrapping it around the joints.*

illusion

Nylon wire is so fine that you can create the illusion that beads are floating around your neck. The crimps in this project are used as stoppers for the beads rather than being fully crimped.

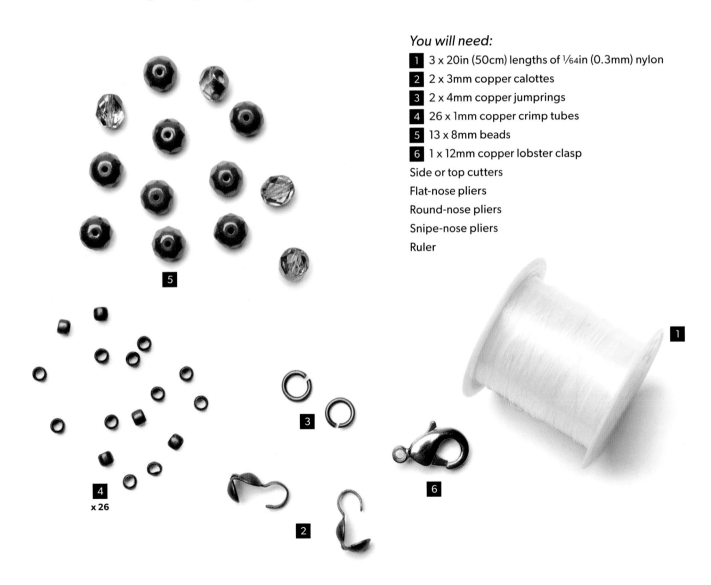

You will need:

1 3 x 20in (50cm) lengths of ¹⁄₆₄in (0.3mm) nylon
2 2 x 3mm copper calottes
3 2 x 4mm copper jumprings
4 26 x 1mm copper crimp tubes
5 13 x 8mm beads
6 1 x 12mm copper lobster clasp
Side or top cutters
Flat-nose pliers
Round-nose pliers
Snipe-nose pliers
Ruler

x 26

Tip Where possible, use smaller beads to avoid the nylon drooping.

1 Cut 3 x 20-in (50cm) lengths of nylon and, holding all the ends together, thread them through the hole on a small calotte. Tie a knot as near to the end of the threads as possible.

2 Slide the calotte along the nylon with your fingers to cover the knot. Using flat-nose pliers, gently squash the two hemispheres together to close the calotte over the knot.

3 Cut off the excess nylon ends and close the calotte's "tail" with round-nose pliers, forming a small eye loop. Link a 4mm jumpring through this eye loop and close.

4 Now that you have made one end of the necklace, you have a more accurate guide to measuring your nylon strands to 16in (40cm) long. Place the strands along a ruler and, starting 2½in (6cm) from the calotte, mark dots every 2½in (6cm) on strand 1 and strand 3 using a pen. Then mark strand 2, starting 3½in (9cm) from the calotte and marking every 2½in (6cm), so that the marks are evenly staggered along the necklace length. Do this for a total of 13½in (34cm), so that you end up with another gap of 2½in (6cm) where you will add the calotte at the other end of the necklace.

5 Thread a crimp tube onto the first nylon thread and squash it flat at the first mark, using flat-nose pliers. Try to keep the nylon thread running through the middle of the crimp.

6 Slide your first bead followed by another crimp tube onto the nylon, so that they sit flush against the first crimp. Squash the crimp tube tightly onto the nylon to secure the bead in place.

7 Repeat steps 5 and 6 until all the beads and crimps are secured on the nylon strands.

8 Repeat steps 1 and 2, adding a calotte to the other end of the necklace. Cut off any excess nylon ends.

9 Using round-nose pliers, close the calotte's "tail" to form an eye loop. Link a lobster clasp onto a 4mm jumpring, link the jumpring through the calotte eye loop and close.

Tip This necklace works best at a short length of about 16in (40cm).

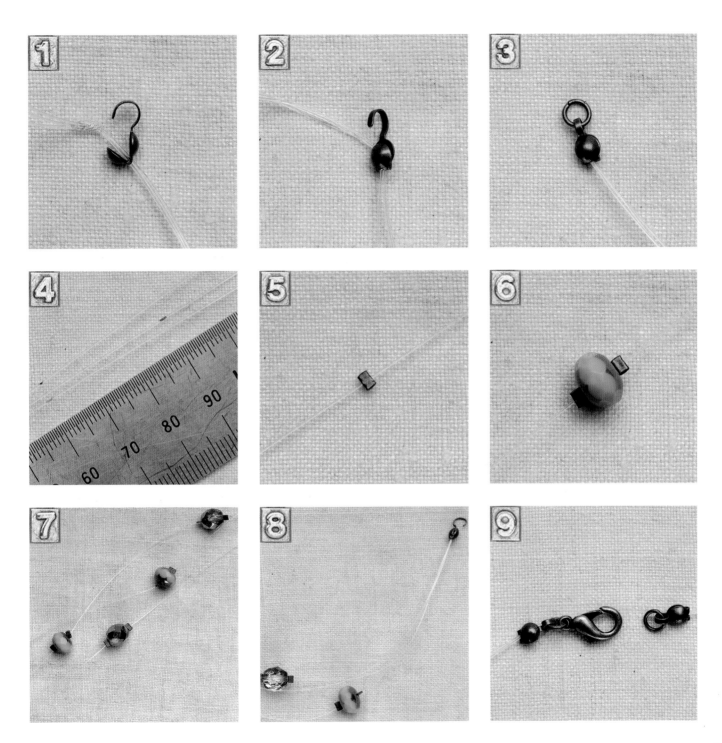

kitty

Adorn your wrist and make a statement with a colorful leather bracelet and cat charms. Team brightly colored leather with cool cat charms to make the perfect piece of jewellery for a trendsetter.

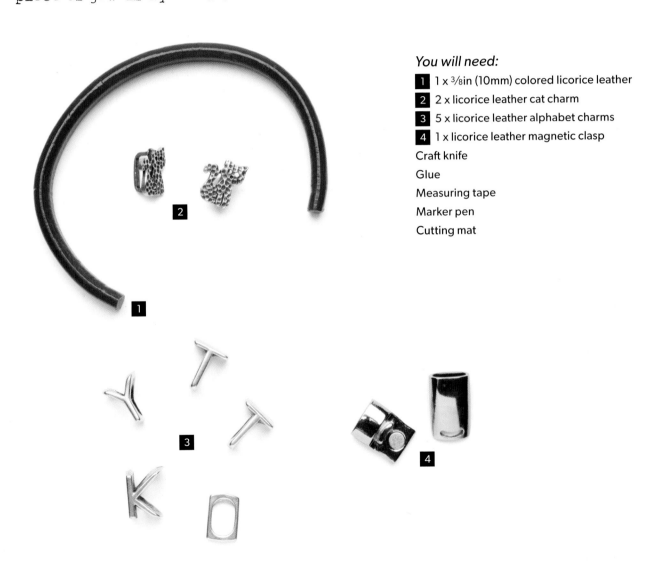

You will need:

1 1 x ³⁄₈in (10mm) colored licorice leather

2 2 x licorice leather cat charm

3 5 x licorice leather alphabet charms

4 1 x licorice leather magnetic clasp

Craft knife

Glue

Measuring tape

Marker pen

Cutting mat

Tip *Licorice leather varies slightly in size so make sure your charms match the size of the leather. If possible buy all the components from the same supplier.*

1 Measure your wrist, allowing a bit of room for movement. Remember that the clasp will add ½in (12mm) to the size.

2 Carefully cut the leather to your required length. Do this on a cutting mat using a craft knife.

3 Take one end of the clasp and place a small amount of glue in the end. Push the leather in as far as it will go. Leave to dry.

4 When the glue has dried, thread on the charms in the order you want them.

5 Take the piece of the clasp that has not been used and place a small amount of glue in the end. As in step 3, push onto the end of the leather as far as you can. Leave to dry.

6 Finally, move the charms around until you are happy with where they sit, then place a tiny dot of glue on the inside to hold each charm in place.

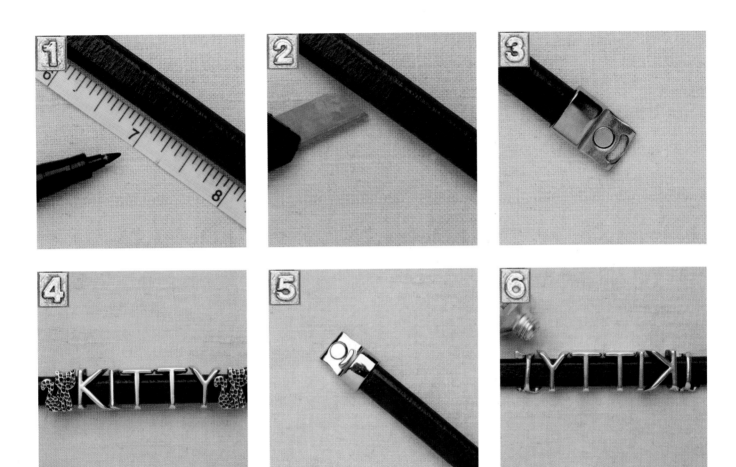

Tip *Alphabet charms are great; you can spell out any word or name. It could be the name of your pet or a person.*

victoriana

This stylish brooch inspired by the Victorian era makes the perfect finishing touch to any outfit. Silhouettes from magazines, photos, drawings, or even cutouts from fabric are all suitable for making this sophisticated brooch.

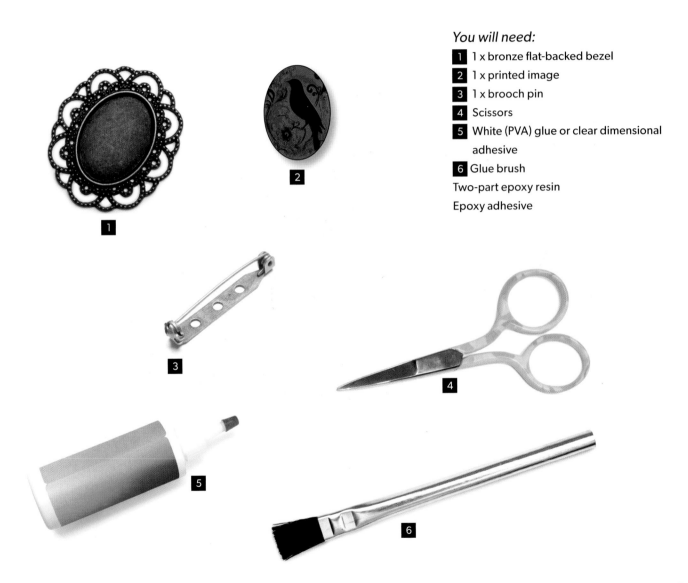

You will need:

1. 1 x bronze flat-backed bezel
2. 1 x printed image
3. 1 x brooch pin
4. Scissors
5. White (PVA) glue or clear dimensional adhesive
6. Glue brush

Two-part epoxy resin

Epoxy adhesive

1 Find an image that you like. Cut it out, and check that it fits into the bezel. If you are using a different image, place the bezel on the image and draw around the inside rim.

2 Paint the front and sides of your image with glue. Leave it to dry and then turn it over and repeat on the back and sides. Do this twice to be sure it is completely sealed.

3 When the image is dry, put a tiny blob of white (PVA) glue or clear dimensional adhesive onto the back of it and press into the bezel so it is completely flat.

4 Mix the two-part epoxy resin (see page 352) and pour into the bezel on top of the image. Leave to dry for at least 24 hours.

5 Mix some epoxy adhesive (see page 351). Cover the brooch pin with glue, and also a vertical line down the middle of the bezel back where you will stick the pin. Make sure the pin runs parallel with your bird image so it is the right way up when attached to clothing.

6 Stick the brooch pin onto the back of the bezel and leave to dry flat for at least 8 hours.

Tip *When using a fabric or paper image, always seal it with white (PVA) glue before pouring the resin into the bezel so that the resin does not damage it.*

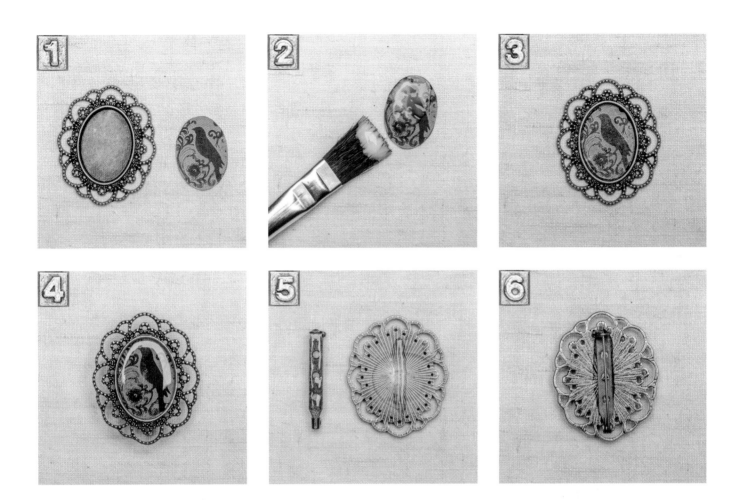

Tip *The key to good results is to store and work with the resin in a warm room. The resin can become cloudy if it gets too cold, and the warmer the room the quicker it cures (hardens).*

spirals

This simple but effective design will give you the confidence to start using wire and creating your own shapes. These earrings show off the wire-wrapped details, and there is always something satisfying about a spiral.

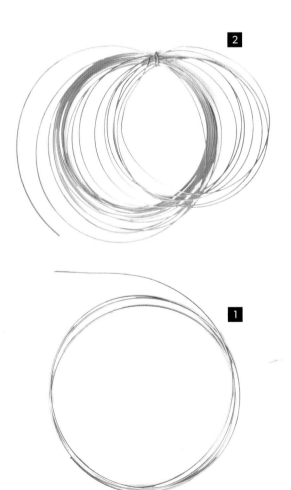

You will need:

1 US 18 gauge (SWG 19, 1mm) silver wire
2 US 22 gauge (SWG 23, 0.6mm) silver wire
    Round-nose pliers
    Snipe-nose pliers
    Side cutters

1 Make an earring hoop of your chosen size (see page 333).

2 Cut off 8in (20cm) of US 18 gauge (SWG 19, 1mm) wire using side cutters. Holding the very end of the wire with round-nose pliers, create a loop large enough for the wire to pass through.

3 Hold the loop with snipe-nose pliers and start to spiral the wire around itself, turning the spiral each time to keep it even.

4 When you have created three spirals, take hold of the other end of the wire at the very tip and bend it back on itself to make a small kink. Squash this kink as tightly as possible, then, holding it flat, start to spiral the wire the other way around the kink. Continue spiralling until you meet the other spiral.

5 Thread the spiral design onto the hoop through the hole in the center of the smaller spiral, keeping the hoop open.

6 Cut off 4in (10cm) of US 22 gauge (SWG 23, 6mm) wire. Hold the wire against part of the hoop, then start to wrap it around the hoop, keeping the wire as tight and even as possible. Keep a count of how many times you wrap it round, so that you can match it on the other side.

7 Use side cutters to cut away the excess wire. If necessary, use snipe-nose pliers to squash the wire coil tightly against the hoop.

8 Repeat steps 6–7 to wrap wire around the other side of the earring hoop. Finally, repeat the process to create the other earring.

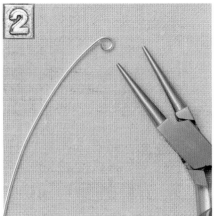

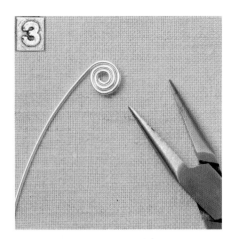

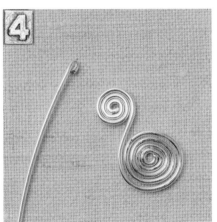

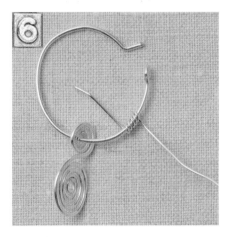

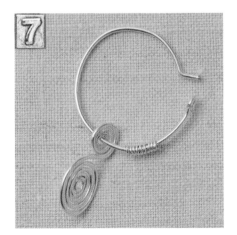

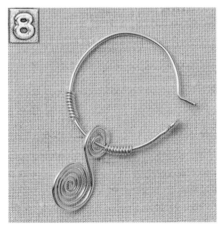

Tip *Experiment with different thicknesses of wire.*

zippy

Like buttons, zippers come in a vast array of wonderful colors, so there is no excuse not to make a necklace to suit any occasion. The length of your zipper will determine the size of the rose.

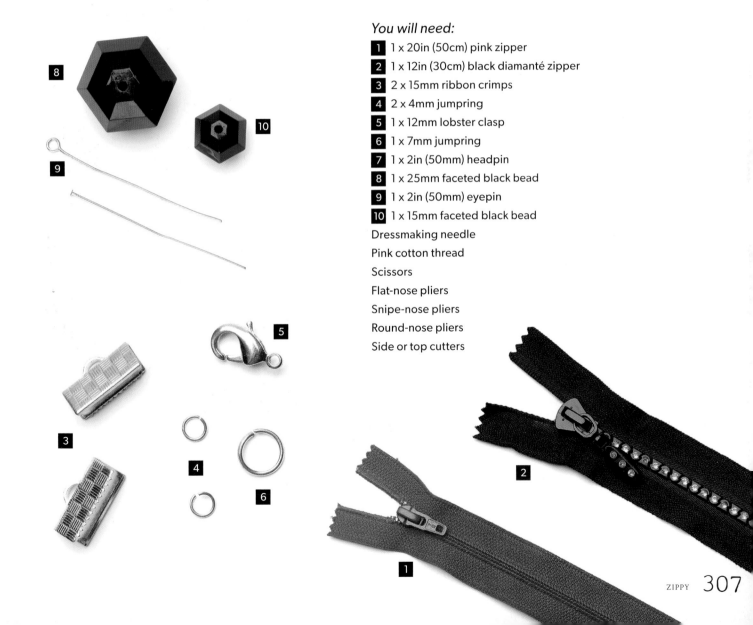

You will need:

1. 1 x 20in (50cm) pink zipper
2. 1 x 12in (30cm) black diamanté zipper
3. 2 x 15mm ribbon crimps
4. 2 x 4mm jumpring
5. 1 x 12mm lobster clasp
6. 1 x 7mm jumpring
7. 1 x 2in (50mm) headpin
8. 1 x 25mm faceted black bead
9. 1 x 2in (50mm) eyepin
10. 1 x 15mm faceted black bead

Dressmaking needle

Pink cotton thread

Scissors

Flat-nose pliers

Snipe-nose pliers

Round-nose pliers

Side or top cutters

1 Unzip the 20in (50cm) pink dress zipper as far as it will go, so that the zipper is still joined but you have two separate halves to work with. Starting from one of the ends without the zipper pull attached, form a tight spiral of a couple of turns. Using a dressmaking needle and matching pink thread, hand sew a couple of stitches to secure the spiral.

2 Form a small section of the zipper into a loop directly next to the stitched spiral, then hand stitch the loop to the spiral.

3 Continue to form loops that overlap each other like the petals of a rose. The loops will naturally become larger as you move around the spiral. Remember to sew a stitch or two at each loop to hold them all in place.

4 When you get to the bottom of the zipper, make sure that the zipper pull is hanging down and doesn't get caught up in a loop and stitched. Now take the second half of the zipper and start to form more loops, continuing around the ones made in steps 2 and 3, again adding a stitch or two as you go.

5 Keeping the black diamanté dress zipper closed, fold the bottom ends in to form a small triangular point. Stitch the zipper right side down to the back of the rose, so that the pink zipper pull is dangling down vertically and the diamantés of the black zipper will be facing vertically when viewed from the front.

6 Unzip the black zipper, so that you have two separate sections. Add a ribbon crimp to each end by sandwiching the zipper ends between the ribbon crimp and then squashing the crimp with flat-nose pliers.

7 Open 1 x4mm jumpring (see page 332) and link on the lobster clasp, then link the jumpring to one ribbon crimp end and close. Open the other 4mm jumpring and add 1 x 7mm jumpring for the "eye" of the clasp; link the 4mm jumpring to the other end of the ribbon crimp and close.

8 Thread a headpin through the 25mm black bead and form a closed eye loop as close to the top of the bead as possible. If the hole of your bead is too big, add a smaller bead first to trap the headpin.

9 Pass the eyepin through the smaller black bead and form an eye loop as close to the top of the bead as possible. Join the two beads together by the eye loops and finally link them onto the pink zipper pull.

Tip *Make sure you stitch at every petal so that the zipper rose doesn't unravel.*

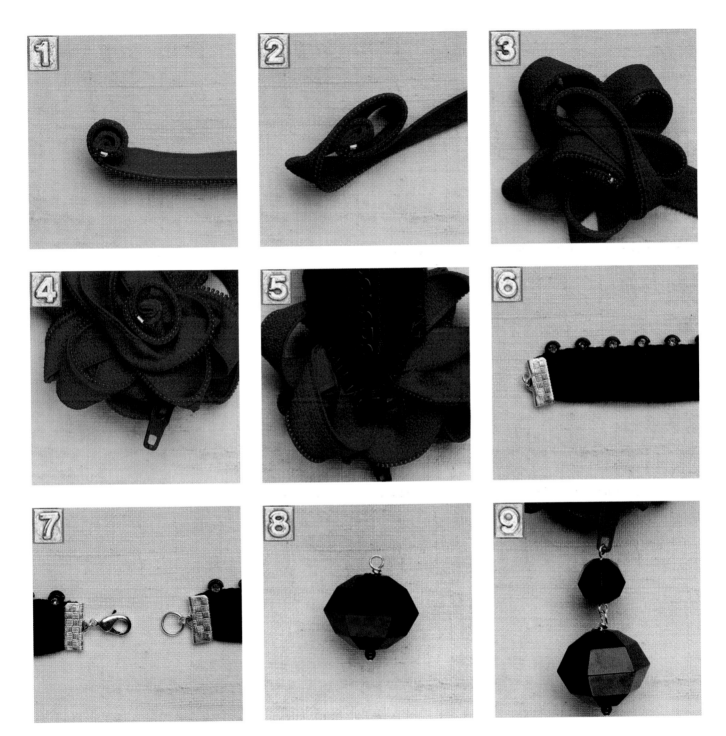

nala

Sparkle like a kitten in these purr-fect ears! There is nothing better than a pair of glittering crystal-bead cat ears to liven up any party outfit and cause a stir.

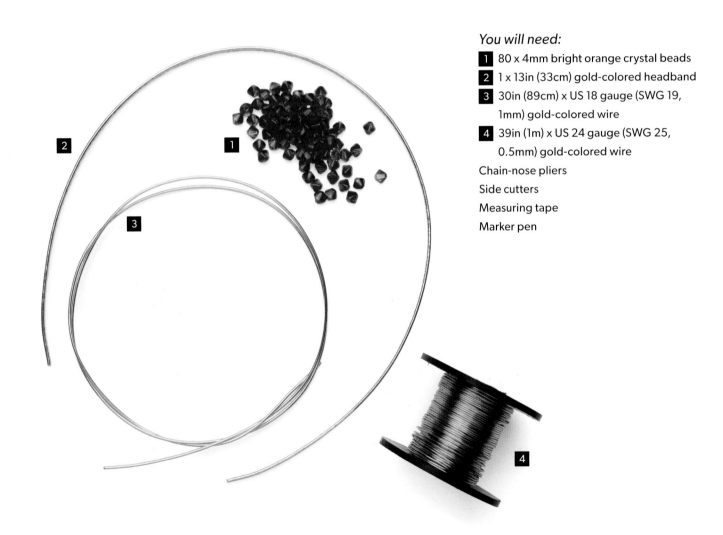

You will need:

1. 80 x 4mm bright orange crystal beads
2. 1 x 13in (33cm) gold-colored headband
3. 30in (89cm) x US 18 gauge (SWG 19, 1mm) gold-colored wire
4. 39in (1m) x US 24 gauge (SWG 25, 0.5mm) gold-colored wire

Chain-nose pliers
Side cutters
Measuring tape
Marker pen

1 Take the measuring tape and marker pen. Measure up from the end of the band 4½in (11.5cm) and make a mark on the band; repeat for the other side. From that mark, measure 2in (50mm) and mark again, and repeat this from the mark on the other side. You should have four marks in total. Don't worry about the marks showing as the wire will cover them all.

2 Take the US 18 gauge (SWG 19, 1mm) wire and, starting at one of the first marks up from the end of the band, wrap the wire around the band five times, so the wire coil ends on the pen mark. The long end on the wire needs to be where the pen mark is.

3 Measure along the wire about 2in (5cm) and bend it back toward the band. Measure another 2in (5cm) and bend again. The wire will want to curve naturally so you should see an ear shape forming.

4 Place the final bend you made in step 3 under the headband and start a coil around the band at the pen mark. Keep coiling until you get to the next pen mark. Try to keep the coil tight to the band and close together. 18 gauge wire is pretty hard so it will take some effort to make it coil nicely.

5 Repeat step 3 for the second ear.

6 Find the final pen mark and coil five times around the band. Snip off any extra wire.

7 Take the US 24 gauge (SWG 25, 0.5mm)wire and coil a couple of times around the base of one of the cat ears.

8 Thread a few crystals onto the wire and coil around the US 18 gauge (SWG 19, 1mm) wire on the opposite side of the ear. Add more crystals and coil around the opposite side again.

9 Keep adding a few crystals at a time and wrap the wire from side to side and up and down until you have a pattern you are happy with. This project used about 40 crystals per ear but you can add more or less as desired. Repeat for the other ear.

Tip *To make your headband sit comfortably behind the ears, bend it into a "U" shape with your fingers.*

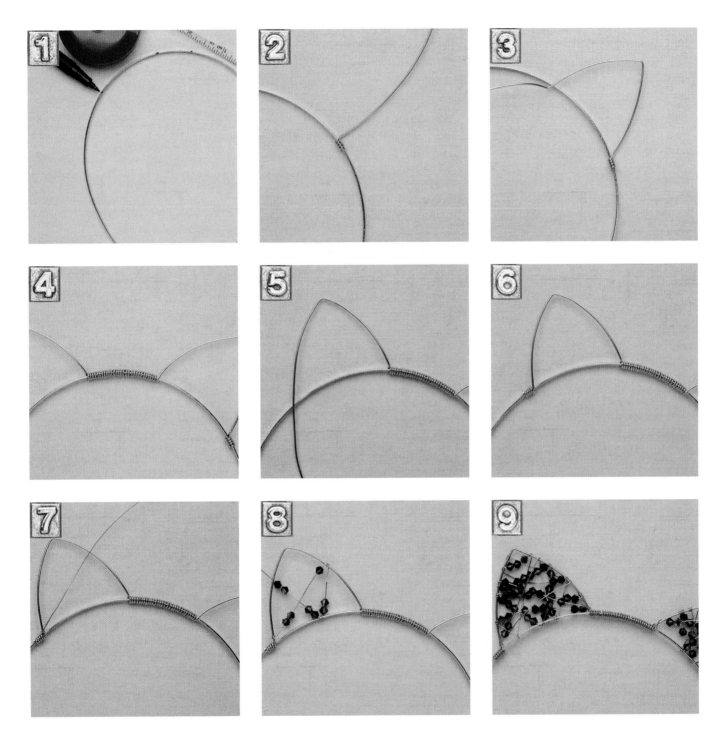

Tools & materials

Pliers

When holding, forming or shaping pieces of jewelry, the most common tools used are pliers. You can get different types that are designed for particular uses. However, even if you have just one pair of multi pliers, you should be able to tackle most jobs.

1 Round-nose pliers

These pliers have round, tapered jaws that start small at the very tip and increase to a larger circumference at the base. They are used for making eyepins, wrapping loops, and shaping wire.

3 Snipe-nose pliers

Sometimes known as chain-nose pliers, these pliers have half-round jaws with flat parallel inside faces that touch. They are also tapered from small at the very tip of the nose to a larger half-round at the base. Their unique shape makes them ideal for holding small jewelry components, opening and closing chain links or jumprings, and shaping wire in general.

2 Flat-nose pliers

These pliers have flat parallel jaws at the top and bottom. They are handy for bending sharp corners or straightening wire, crimping flat ribbon crimps, and holding, opening, and closing jumprings and other small components.

4 Crimping pliers

Crimping pliers come in a variety of sizes and it is important to have the correct size jaw for the crimps that you most commonly use. The jaw has two sections: the back forms your crimp tube into a curve, trapping the contents; and the front folds the crimp in half, securing everything in place.

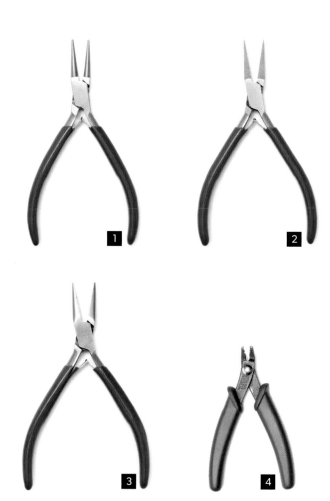

Cutters

There are various types and sizes of cutters used in jewelry making. To simplify their uses, cutters are used for cutting thin materials and wire, snips for cutting sheet material, and scissors for cutting paper and fabric.

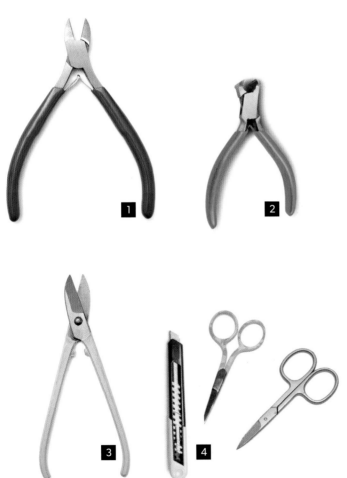

1 Side cutters

Similar to end cutters, but the cutter runs along the side of these. Use the flat side against the end of the wire you are keeping, as it will leave you with a neater cut edge. The tips are handy for getting into small spaces such as individual links of small chain.

3 Wire snips

Snips are often seen as a pair of scissors for sheet metal, but they are also useful for trimming ribbon or leather. Be aware, though, that they will leave a mark on the surface when cutting.

2 End cutters

The cutter is at the end of this tool and is suitable for cutting thin materials, chain, and wire. The design of this tool lets you get right up close to your design to snip off any excess wire and leave you with a flush finish.

4 Scissors and craft knife

General-purpose scissors should have a fine, long nose so that you can reach into small areas, and be sharp so that you can accurately cut fabric and paper. A craft knife is handy for getting into those trickier curved designs and small places where scissors may be more awkward.

Adhesives

When making jewelry, use glues that are suited to the purpose.
Use adhesives in a well-ventilated area.

1 Epoxy glue

Two-part adhesives mix together to form an adhesive of a thicker consistency that sets hard. These are useful where you do not want glue to run onto other surfaces. Where possible use ones that dry clear, giving a professional finish.

2 White (PVA) glue

This is great for painting onto surfaces as it dries completely clear and rigid. This makes it useful for stiffening fabrics or sealing papers prior to using resin.

3 Superglue

A very handy resource for sealing knots and ideal for use on all types of beads and threads, although it can react with metals, illusion cord and melt materials, so should only be used for certain tasks.

4 Glue gun

A glue gun heats up sticks of glue to melting point so that you can squeeze blobs of hot glue onto certain surfaces—such as metal and plastic—where other thinner adhesives may not be as effective. Be careful because the glue can get really hot.

5 E6000

This is industrial thick glue used to coat wire to stop sharp edges from scratching skin and for sticking shrink plastic to combs and metal findings.

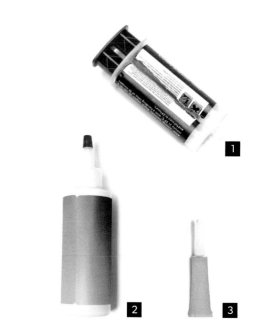

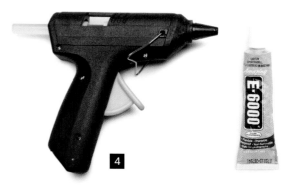

Miscellaneous tools

All of these tools are used in the projects in this book; many of them are nonspecialist items available in hardware and craft stores.

1 Spacers

Used to get a consistent thickness when rolling out clay, spacers are plastic bars that come in a set of different thicknesses. Put them either side of the clay while you roll it out. A stack of playing cards works just as well.

2 Teflon sheet

Sold in most cook stores, Teflon sheet is nonstick and is used to roll clay out on. It can be cut to size.

3 Tape measure

Whether you're working with wire or fabric, a tape measure is essential for measuring your materials to obtain accurate lengths for your design.

Rollers

For use with polymer clay and metal clay, rollers are a hollow or solid plastic tube that you use to roll clays out to a thin sheet. You can make your own by cutting a small section of the type of tubing that is widely available in building supplies stores in the plumbing aisle.

5 Glue brushes

These are short-handled paintbrushes used for applying multipurpose white (PVA) glue and varnish.

6 Emery paper/Needle file

This can be used to soften any sharp edges on pieces of wire, especially if they are to be used to make jewelry findings. You can also use a nail file or needle file.

7 Ring mandrel

This is a tapered cylindrical former with measurements marked evenly along it that correspond to ring sizes. Place one of your existing rings onto it to see what size your finger is. Wrap wire at this point to guarantee a ring that fits you perfectly.

8 Bead board

This is a great tool for planning the length of necklaces. The channels have measurements on them and by placing your beads in the channels you can see exactly how many you will need. The compartments in the middle are for holding the findings that you will be using for that particular piece.

9 Bead mat

A cheaper equivalent to the bead board, this cushioned soft mat stops your beads and findings from rolling around. It does not have any compartments in it.

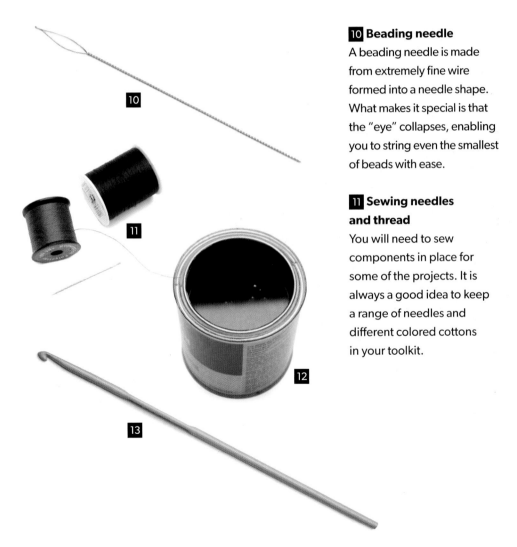

10 Beading needle

A beading needle is made from extremely fine wire formed into a needle shape. What makes it special is that the "eye" collapses, enabling you to string even the smallest of beads with ease.

11 Sewing needles and thread

You will need to sew components in place for some of the projects. It is always a good idea to keep a range of needles and different colored cottons in your toolkit.

12 Varnish

Clear polyurethane creates a tough protective topcoat for paper decoupage, wood, or beads.

13 Crochet hook

Crochet hooks are available from craft shops, markets, or online. Different sizes will create different effects. A small hook (US10–B/1:1–2.25mm:UK4–13) will produce close, delicate work whereas a larger hook (USD/3–G/6: 3.25–4mm: UK10–8) will produce more loopy work.

Marker pens/nail varnish

Marker pens are easier to see when putting measurements onto wire, nylon, or steel-coated threads than ordinary pen. Nail varnish can also be used, especially when coloring the ends of headpins to give a unique touch to any design.

Findings

Findings are all the items you use to make up jewelry that are not beads, pendants, or charms.

1 Bead cups
These are slightly domed shapes with a hole in the center, which fit over the ends of beads to add extra decoration.

2 Jumprings
A jumpring is a single ring of wire that is used to join pieces together; they come in every size you can think of and also in many colors.

3 Earwires
Earwires come in various styles, from a simple "U" shape with a loop, to ones with a bead and coil finish. The loop is opened to take the earring piece.

4 Headpins and eyepins
These are pieces of wire with a flat or ball end (headpin) or a loop at the end (eyepin). Thread a bead on the wire and make a loop at the open end to secure the bead in place. Eyepins can be linked together to make a chain.

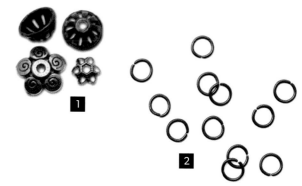

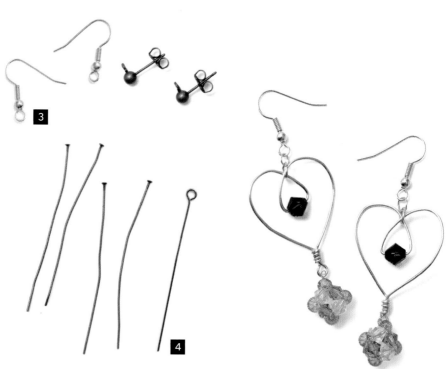

5 Posts and backs

Posts come with a bead and open loop or with a blank disk front. The disk style is used with glue. They are often supplied with butterfly/scroll backs.

6 Brooch pin and kilt pin

This is a brooch pin on a bar that has holes to attach it to the piece of jewelry. It can be sewn on, attached with wire, or glued. Kilt pins have loops at the bottom that you can hang beads and charms from them.

7 Bezel blanks

These are flat plates with a shallow wall around the sides, either with a loop on one end to attach to a chain or attached to cufflink backs, ring shanks, or bracelets. They can be filled with resin or clay. They come in a variety of shapes.

8 Blanks

These are items such as rings, cufflinks, or buttons that have a flat plate to which you can glue your decoration. You can get blanks on ring shanks, pendants, cufflinks, and as buttons.

9 Noodle tubes

These are tubes that come in a variety of sizes and straight or curved shapes to allow stringing material to pass through them, thus creating decorative spaces between beads.

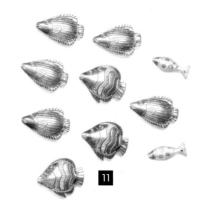

10 Calottes

Calottes are small, hinged cups with a loop on one cup (these can be open loops or closed rings) and a hole in the middle of the hinge to take thread. They work by holding a seed bead or crimp bead inside the cup with the thread coming out of hole in the hinge to make the ends of piece look neater. To close them gently press the two cups together. The loop is for attaching the calotte to jumprings or clasps.

11 Crimp tubes and covers

This is a more elaborate version of a calotte, consisting of a little tube that you crimp using crimping pliers (see page 316) and a cover that you wrap over it to finish it off.

12 Magnetic clasp

These are great for bracelets when making for anyone who finds opening and closing clasps difficult. Keep in mind that magnets will attach to some base metals like plated chains.

13 Trigger clasp

These are also known as a lobster or parrot clasp. These are the most widely used clasps on the market. Some come with a jumpring attached and they vary in size and style.

14 Toggle clasp

A great choice when making the clasp a feature in your design, toggles have a loop on one end and a bar that fits through the loop to attach to the other end.

15 Ribbon/cord crimps

These are available in various different sizes and shapes to match the width of the ribbon, cord, leather thong or feather that you want to attach it to. When closed with pliers, they securely grasp the end of the material and have a loop attached so you can easily connect them to your design.

16 T-bar and loop fittings

The T-bar is a type of fastener. It is a straight bar, with a loop halfway along the underside for a jumpring to attach to the end of a chain. The loop is attached to the other end of the chain and is large enough for the T-bar to pass through but not to fall back out.

Basic materials

You will need a range of beads, pendants, charm, fabric, and hair accessories to make the projects in this book.

1 Beads

There is such a large variety of beads available, from tiny seed beads to large, handmade lampwork glass ones. Beads can be made from plastic, wood, metal, glass, resin, or crystal. When selecting beads, it's good to start with a theme, such as cats, then match different styles of beads together using a color palette.

2 Charms

Charms can be metal, plastic, wood, or pretty much any material. The term "charm" is often given to a jewelry item that has a hole or loop at the top to attach it to the jewelry.

3 Buttons

Shaped buttons are great for jewelry as they come with premade holes to attach them to jumprings or wire.

4 Self-cover buttons

Mainly used for upholstery, these buttons can also be highly versatile as jewelry components. They come in many different sizes and you can easily cover them in patterned fabrics to enhance your designs.

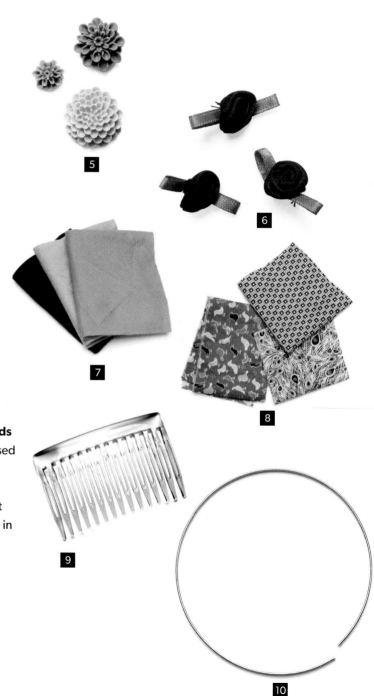

5 Resin shapes

Flower shapes cast in resin come with flat backs for sticking to blanks, such as rings, cufflinks, or button backs.

6 Fabric/ribbon flowers

Tiny ribbon flowers are available from craft stores in many colors and styles. If you're lucky you might be able to find some beautiful vintage silk flowers or try department stores and garden centers to find new ones.

7 Felt/patterned textiles

Use fancy fabric to cover beads and buttons or create whole charm designs with leather or felt. You can always find cheap offcuts of leather in fabric and craft stores or you can scour thrift shops and recycle old textiles.

8 Paper

Collect beautiful wrapping paper, images from books and magazines, and old sheet music to use for collage and decoupage or as inspiration for your designs.

9 Hair combs

Clear combs are good for jewelry making as you can embellish them with wire and beads or glue a feature piece on the front.

10 Hairbands or tiara bands

Round tiara bands can be used to sit on top of the head or gently bent out to make a U-shape for a hairband to sit behind the ears. They come in silver or gold colors and are made of a strip of metal.

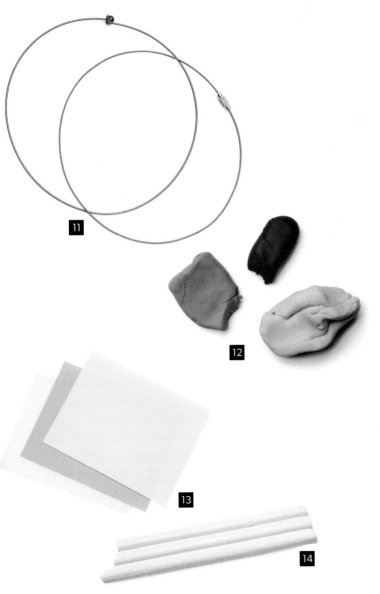

11 Choker
Ready-made necklaces are widely available; they come in different sizes and most have a screw clasp. The wire choker style is usually made from steel wire coated in nylon, which is then colored.

12 Polymer clay
Polymer clay is a plastic modeling compound that is soft and pliable until it is baked in a standard oven. It comes in a large variety of colors and brands; each brand has a different baking temperature, so check the manufacturer's instructions before using. Polymer clay also comes in great special effects, such as metallic colors and even one that glows in the dark!

13 Oil-based modeling clay
Soft, pliable oil-based modeling clay (Plastilina or Plasticine) that doesn't harden is handy for using as a prop to push objects into to hold them steady while you work on them.

14 Shrink plastic
This is paper-thin plastic that shrinks in a standard oven and becomes seven times smaller and seven times thicker than its original size as well as more rigid. It can be colored and cut into any shape with scissors. You can also create shapes in it using paper punches.

Stringing materials

When making your jewelry, there are various stringing options you might want to consider.

1 Chain

There are many styles of chain and a variety of colors available. Fine chains are good for hanging pendants and large-link chains are good for making charm bracelets or when adding beads to the individual links.

2 Wire

Wire comes in a large range of sizes. Often referred to in the USA by gauge and in the UK by millimeters, conversion charts are widely available on the Internet. If buying plated wire, look for a non-tarnish variety.

3 Suede/leather/waxed cord

All of these cords or thongs are usually sold by the meter and are used to create friendship-style bracelets and necklaces. Charms and beads can easily be threaded onto single strands or, if multiple cords are plaited together, charms can be attached using jumprings.

4 Ribbon

Ribbon comes in many different materials, including satin, velvet, and silk, and is available in all colors, designs, and widths. It can be used for decoration but is also great for using in place of, or alongside, chain to create necklaces and bracelets. For strength and rigidity, use grosgrain ribbon, which is woven, has a ribbed appearance, and tends to feel thicker than most ribbons.

5 Elastic

Elastic comes in many varieties. You can thread beads and charms onto clear or colored elastic thread to create gorgeous bracelets and necklaces that stretch and slide on and off easily. There are thread-covered elastics (more commonly used in sewing) and also multistrand elastics, both of which are excellent for tying knots in, as the way they are made means the elastic is not slippery. They are, however, easier to snap, so you may need to use extra lengths for doubling up when stringing.

6 Illusion cord

The other variety of elastic is extremely durable, shiny, and transparent. Being transparent, it is often used where you do not want the stringing material to interfere visually with the design; this is often referred to as illusion elastic or cord. However, its surface is slippery and therefore is best crimped rather than knotted, although you can add a drop of glue to any knots.

7 Nylon-coated wire

Often referred to as "tigertail," this is constructed of several fine steel wires bound together in a nylon coating. It is stronger than nylon, but cannot be successfully knotted; ideally, you should use crimps to add any fixings. As it comes in a variety of thicknesses and colors, you can often make this form of stringing a feature of your design.

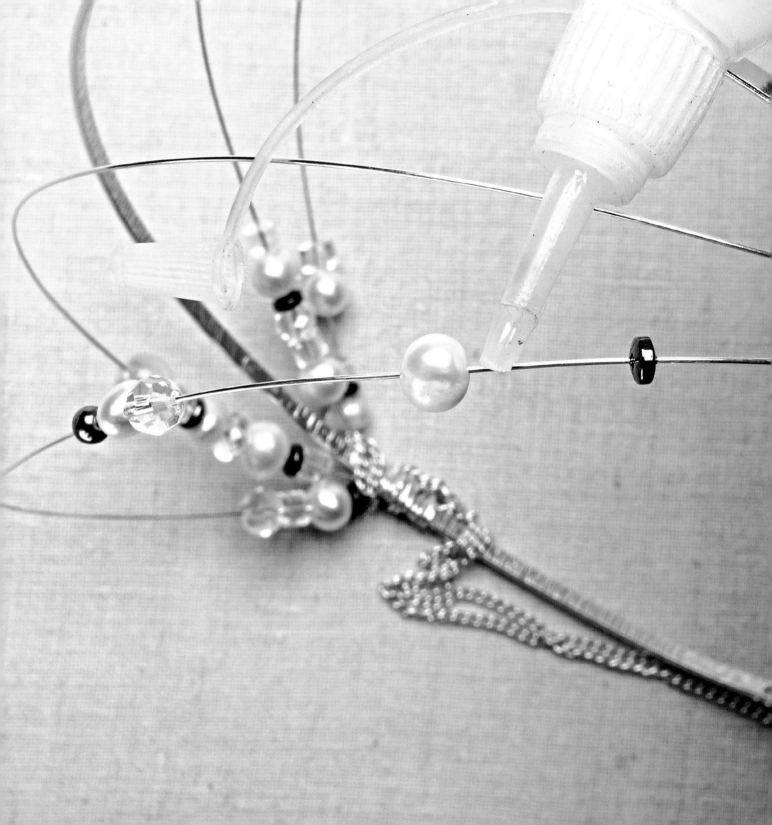

Techniques

Findings

Here is how to use and make some
of the small components that make up your pieces of jewelry.

Opening and closing jumprings

To make sure that jumprings shut securely, it is important to
know how to open and close them correctly.

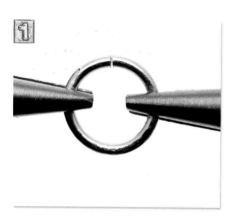

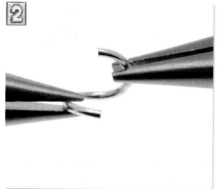

1 Grip the jumpring between two pairs
of pliers. The opening should be
centered at the top.

2 Twist one hand toward you and the
other hand away—this will open
the ring but still keep it round.
Reverse the action to close.

Making earring hoops

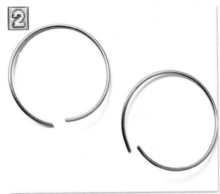

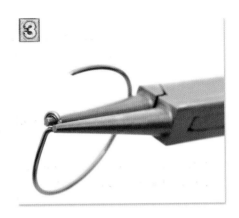

1 Coil round wire twice around a cylindrical former, such as a marker pen. The size of the former will determine how large the hoop will be. An average size is approximately ¾in (20mm).

2 Cut through the coils to create two separate hoops of the same size.

3 With round-nose pliers, grip the very end of the wire on one of the hoops and turn it to form a small closed loop.

4 Hold the other end of the wire with flat parallel nose pliers and bend it approximately 45 degrees so that it fits through the loop. Once you have fastened the hoop, you may need to tweak the shape of the hoop with your fingers to make it round again.

Making a spiral

An attractive spiral works nicely to decorate pieces instead of using a simple headpin.

1 Take a length of wire and, with round-nose pliers, bend the very tip around in a loop.

2 Place the loop flat in the jaws of chain-nose pliers and push the wire against the loop.

3 Work round in a circle, moving the loop in the chain-nose pliers. Allow the wire to coil around the outside of the loop to make your spiral.

Making eyepins

1 Thread the beads or jewelry items onto the eyepin. Using pliers make a right-angle bend in the wire that extends from the end bead. Make the bend as close to the bead as possible.

2 For a large eye, use wire snips to cut off all but ⅜in (10mm) of wire. To make a smaller eye, cut it to a length of approximately ¼–⁹⁄₃₂in (6–7mm).

3 Hold the wire in the jaws of some round-nose pliers. Choose an area on the jaw that will give you the size of the eye you require. Then, roll your wrist, twisting the wire into a half coil. Release the wire and move the pliers around the coil before regripping it. Continue to roll the coil to form a P-shape eye. Use flat-nose pliers to center the eye above the bead.

Split rings

A split ring is a small coil of wire used when a more secure connection is required.

1 To open a split ring, slide the point of the split ring pliers between the coils of the ring.

2 Slide the end of the ring onto the jumpring, eyepin, clasp, or wrapped loop that you wish to link it up with.

3 Turn the ring until it is securely linked with the item. The spring will close when you reach the central loop in the ring.

Making split rings

1 Split rings are made in the same way as jumprings, the only difference is when you come to cut them. First, wrap three coils of wire around a round object.

2 Cut the first and third coil of wire so that the ring has a half coil of wire at the start and end with a full ring of wire in the center.

simple and wrapped loops

Loops have a multitude of functions in making
jewelry so making them properly is a skill worth mastering.

Making a simple loop

A simple (sometimes called open) loop can be opened and closed to
allow it to be attached and detached as desired.

1 Thread your chosen bead onto a
headpin or eyepin.

2 Bend the wire to a right angle against
the bead.

3 Snip off to ⁵⁄₁₆in (8mm) or leave more
wire if you need a big loop. Hold the
end of the wire in round-nose pliers
and roll back toward the bead to
create the loop.

Making a wrapped loop

A wrapped or closed loop is very secure. Once an item has been attached this way it cannot be easily removed unless it is cut off.

1 Thread your chosen bead onto a headpin or eyepin.

2 Hold the pin against the bead with a pair of round-nose pliers and bend the wire above the pliers to a right angle.

3 Move the pliers to the top of the right angle and bend the wire all the way around the pliers until it sits by the bead.

4 Thread the loop onto the component you are attaching it to, e.g. a chain.

5 Hold the loop in the round-nose pliers' jaws with the chain away from the bead and wrap the end of the pin around the stem above the bead.

6 Wrap around until the wire meets the bead and snip off any excess wire.

Half-wrapping

This is a pretty Art-Nouveau style of wirework that's practical too as it holds the beads in place without having to use glue. Experiment with where you place the beads to create lovely berry-like tendrils to incorporate into tiaras and combs for a natural look.

Half-wrapping beads

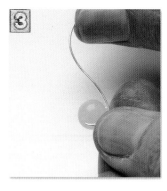

1 Thread your chosen bead onto a length of US 23 gauge (SWG 24, 0.6mm) wire and hold it where you'd like it to sit.

2 Take the wire half way round the bead to the other hole so that the bead is half-wrapped.

3 Using your thumb and forefinger, smooth out a nice curve in the wire next to the bead for about 1in (2.5cm).

4 Add another bead, secure with a half-wrap as before, and carry on.

Fastenings

Crimps, calottes and cord ends are used to join stringing materials such as illusion elastic or nylon-coated wire to findings and clasps in places where knots cannot be used. They are an extremely secure and professional-looking fastening.

Using calottes

  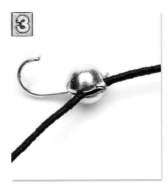 

1 Thread the end of your stringing material through the hole in the center of the calotte.

2 Either slide a crimp tube over the end of the stringing material and crimp it or tie a knot or two so that the stringing material cannot pass back through the hole. Add a drop of glue if you are using slippery material.

3 Slide the calotte up to the crimp or knot and, using flat-nose pliers, gently squeeze the two hemispheres together so that they close over the crimp or knot.

4 The calotte has a little tail of wire. This can be formed into an eye loop so that it can be attached to other findings. Cut away any excess thread that is not required.

Using crimping pliers

1 Thread a crimp tube onto your stringing material, then pass the thread through the finding and back through the crimp tube. Slide the tube along so that it is close to the finding.

2 Hold the crimp tube in the crescent-shaped section of the crimping pliers and squash the crimp tube into a curved shape.

3 Finish the crimping process by moving the now curved crimp tube to the front circular section of the crimping pliers, folding the crimp in half.

Attaching a cord end

There are lots of different styles to choose from so pick one to complement the piece you are making.

1 Place the end of the cord level with the edge of the cord end by the loop. Using pliers, bend one edge against the cord.

2 Now press the opposite side over on top of the side that is already against the cord. Press the edge from the middle or it will not bend level.

3 Use the pliers to make sure the tube you have created is even and that the cord end looks neat. Finally, give a good squeeze to make sure the end is secure.

Finishing off wire

It might seem boring but finishing off your work neatly is quite important so your designs will look tidy and won't scratch you when you put them on! Practice wrapping the wire as tight as you can for a professional finish.

Tidying the wire ends

   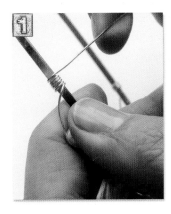

1 When you've completed your design, wrap the wire three times around the tiara base, comb, or slide: keep it as close together and tight to the base as you can.

2 Using the flat side of your snips, cut the wire closely: try and cut it half way down the depth of the base or at the back of the slide to avoid sharp ends on the edge.

3 Squeeze the wrapped end flat to the base/comb/slide with your flat-nose pliers to make sure it's really snug.

4 Feel with your fingers to see if the end still feels sharp: if it does, just gently file the end with a needle or nail file. Be careful though as you can file silver or gold plating off quite easily.

Crochet

If you can already crochet with wool, you're a step ahead here.
Don't worry if you can't though because it's just as easy
to learn to crochet with wire as it stays put!

Chain stitch

1 Make a simple slip knot in the yarn. Use the hook to pull the yarn through the knot to create a loop.

2 Pull the loop up snugly but not too tightly. This is the first stitch in the chain. Insert the hook through this loop, pick up the yarn on the other side.

3 Pull the yarn through the original loop to create the second chain stitch.

4 Repeat steps 2 and 3 to create a chain.

Tip *Join the chain into a ring by hooking the yarn through the first chain stitch.*

Double crochet

1 Begin with a foundation chain, which is two stitches longer than needed, then wind the yarn once around the hook and insert the hook into the third chain stitch from the hook. You will now have three stitches on the hook.

2 Pick up the yarn with the hook and pull it through the first two stitches on the hook.

3 You will now have two stitches on the hook. Pick up the yarn again and pull through those remaining two stitches.

4 There will now be just one stitch left on the hook. The first double crochet stitch is complete. Repeat steps 1–3 for as many stitches as required.

Sewing

These basic hand-sewing techniques will help you finish your projects with flair.

Running stitch

Running stitch is the simplest hand stitch, and it can also be used to create lovely decorative edges on your projects. For the neatest results, try to make all of your stitches the same length.

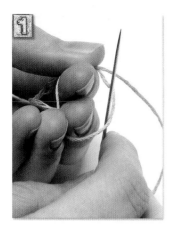

1 Thread your needle and knot the tail end.

2 Pull the needle and thread through the back of your fabric.

3 Now pass the needle in and out of your fabric at even intervals.

4 Repeat until you reach the required number of stitches.

Backstitch

Backstitch creates a neat run of stitches to reinforce your projects, as well as giving them an attractive finish. It's similar to a basic sewing machine stitch, without all the carry on!

 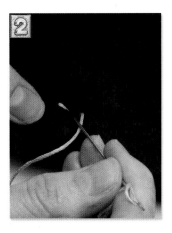 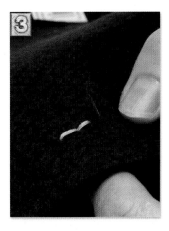 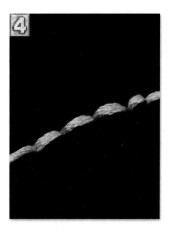

1 Thread your needle and knot the tail end. Make one running stitch. Push the needle up through the fabric one space to the right.

2 Finish the stitch by pushing the needle back into the fabric at the point it was first pulled through, and push to the back.

3 Push the needle up through the fabric one space to the right to make further stitches.

4 Repeat this process until you have the required number of stitches.

Sewing blanket stitch

Any time you are using felt and sewing in a project, blanket stitch is a strong stitch to neaten an edge or to create folds for petals.

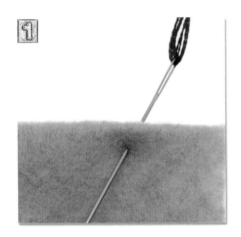

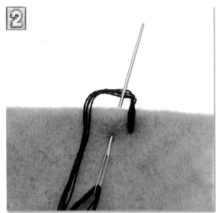

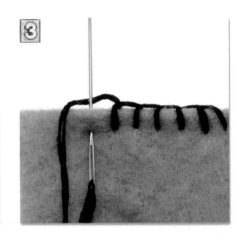

1 Thread a needle with thread about 18in (46cm) long and knot it at the end. Pull the needle through your felt about ⅛in (2mm) down from the edge of the felt or fold. Pull the thread through to the knot.

2 Stay on the same side (opposite side to the knot) and push the needle through about ⅛in (2mm) along from the first stitch, staying level. Loop the thread under the needle and pull gently, so the thread sits on the edge or fold of the felt.

3 Working from the same side the entire time, repeat step 2. Move along the fold or edge ⅛in (2mm) each time, staying at a level of ⅛in (2mm) down from the edge or fold. When you have finished the row of stitching, finish off with a double knot.

Sewing leather

As leather is so dense it is very difficult to sew it using an ordinary needle. It is best to use a special leather needle—which has a chiseled head and very sharp point—combined with a thick, waxed thread. When pushing the needle through, be sure to protect your fingers by using a thick thimble.

Knots

In many different cultures and countries, the craft of knot tying has been passed down through the ages. The Japanese, for example, have used knots for centuries. Many of their traditional knots symbolize love, happiness, good health, even death.

Overhand knot

This simple knot will hold particularly well, especially when painted with nail varnish once it's tied.

1 With an overhand knot the aim is to get the knot as tight as possible against the beads so that the elastic cord doesn't show through. If the knot is chunky, once tied it can be covered with a ribbon or charm.

2 Line up the two ends of the elastic, making sure that they are both the same length. If they are uneven, slide some of the beads along the cord until they are even. Stretch the cords out while holding the beads in place with your other hand.

3 Loop the two ends of the elastic cord around the pointer finger of the other hand and pass the ends through the loop. Slip your finger out, pulling the knot tight up against the beads.

4 Tie a second knot as close to the first as possible. Paint the knot with nail varnish before snipping off the excess cord. Pull the knot back through the closest bead to hide it.

Buttons and bows

These inexpensive techniques will add interesting details to your designs. You can choose from a whole range of fabric and styles to create your own look.

Covering buttons with fabric

Self-cover buttons are available in all craft stores and are so easy to use that it is definitely worth having a go! Make sure you buy the metal buttons that require no tool. These buttons come in various sizes but the technique is always the same.

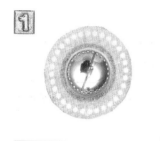

1 Place the button face down on your fabric, draw a circle ⅜in (1cm) bigger all the way around the button and cut out the fabric circle.

2 Place the button front face down on the wrong side of the material. Then fold the fabric over the sides of the button and secure by hooking onto the teeth inside the rim. If you are using bulky fabric you should moisten it to help keep the edges smooth.

3 Keep going until all the fabric is secured and the edges are smooth.

4 Place the button back the loop with the ridge facing down and use your fingers to snap it into place. Now turn the button over and it should be neatly covered and ready to use!

Making a bow

Learn how to make your own bows so you have the perfect size and color for your designs. For the Crystal project (see page 274) you need about 8¾in (22cm) of ribbon to make a good-size bow, but you can change the length of the ribbon according to the size of bow you would like.

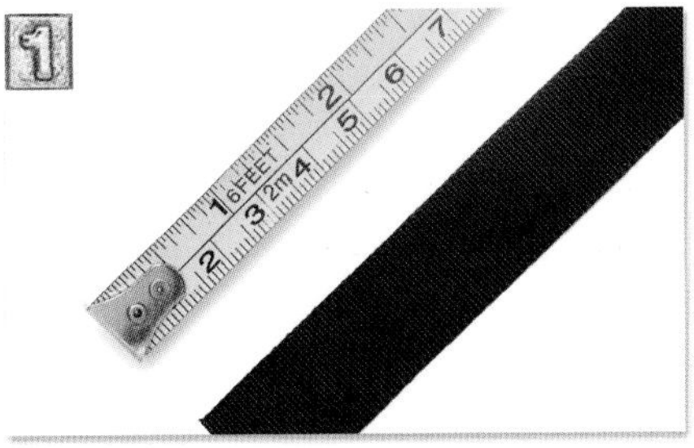

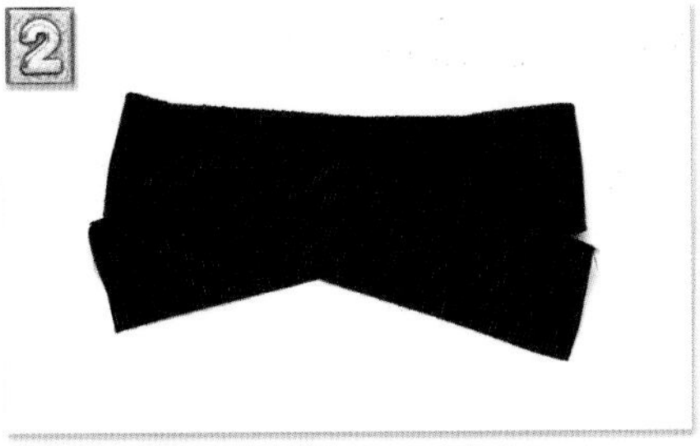

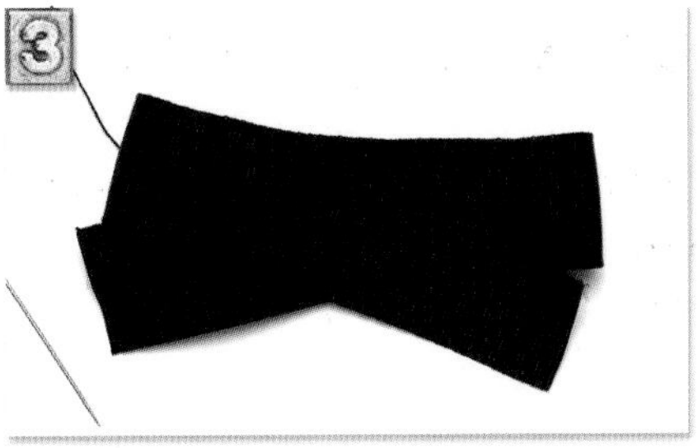

1 Find the center of the ribbon and hold it here.

2 Create a loop on both sides of the center of the ribbon with tails crossing over each other to create an 'X' shape.

3 Using a needle and black thread, put a stitch through the middle of the bow, making sure you go through the front of the ribbon and the two pieces behind it.

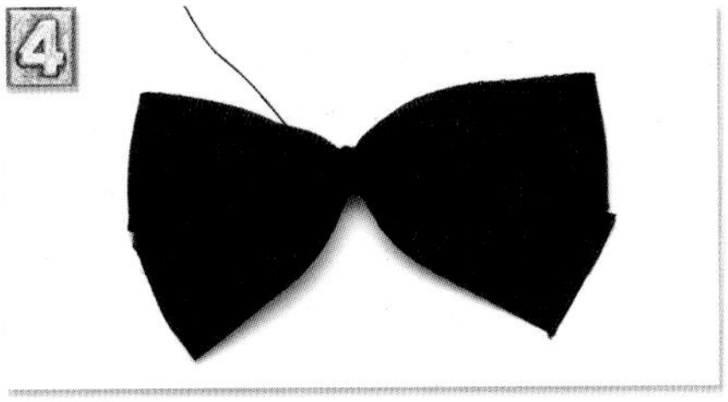

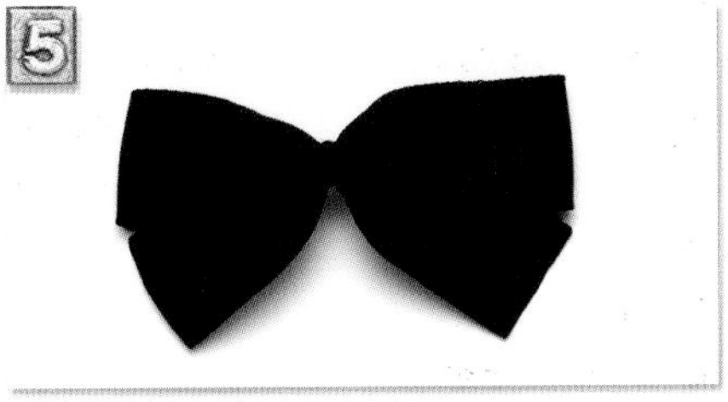

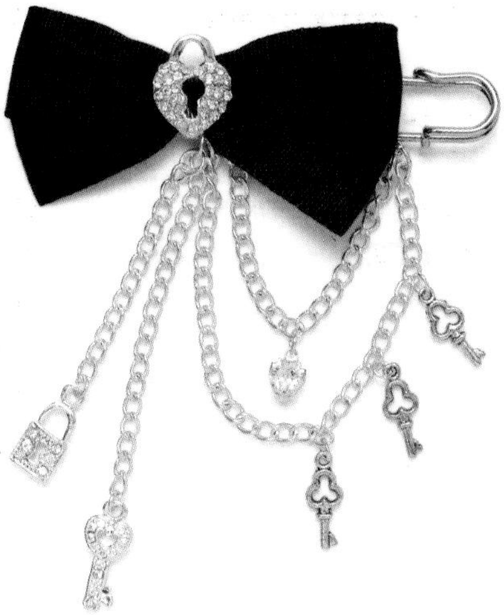

4 Keeping the needle on the thread, wrap the thread around the middle of the bow about six times, pulling it in tightly to create the finished bow appearance.

5 Stitch through the middle of the bow again and tie a secure knot. Use a lighter to seal the ends of the ribbon to prevent fraying. Light the flame and hold each end of the ribbon close enough to it for it to melt slightly.

shrink plastic

This amazing plastic sheet shrinks to 50 percent of its original size when baked in the oven and becomes a strong plastic shape. You can cut it into any shape, color it, paint it, stamp onto it with inks, and print images onto it.

How to use shrink plastic

Regular shrink film is fine for most methods and comes in black and matte as well. Buy special Inkjet shrink film for printing images from the computer (this comes in white and clear).

  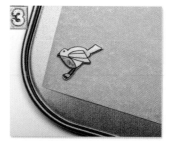 

1 If you will be coloring the plastic, sand the surface with medium-weight emery paper in a crisscross pattern. Then trace, draw, or print your design onto the shrink plastic 50 percent bigger than you want it to be. Cut it out with scissors and use a hole punch to make any holes that you need.

2 Preheat your oven to 350–400°F (180–200°C). Line a baking sheet with parchment paper (baking paper), place your plastic designs on it, and cover them with another piece of parchment paper.

3 Bake in the oven for 2–3 minutes. The plastic will curl up as it bakes and then flatten out again. Do not remove from the oven until the piece is flat.

4 When it is first removed from the oven the plastic will still be pliable but very hot! Wearing gloves, use a spatula to flatten out any slightly curled corners.

Epoxy adhesive

One advantage to epoxy adhesive is that it has a long working time,
meaning that parts can be repositioned for up to 90 minutes. When it does set it is extremely
strong and no other adhesive is as good as this for gluing metal findings to your designs.

How to mix epoxy adhesive

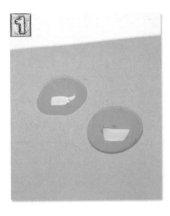   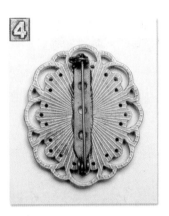

1 Squeeze equal amounts of the resin and hardener next to each other onto a clean disposable surface such as a piece of paper or cardboard.

2 Using a mixing stick, scrape the resin and hardener together into the middle and mix thoroughly for at least 30 seconds until they are well mixed.

3 Make sure both of the surfaces you will be gluing are clean and dry, and for ultimate bonding slightly sand both surfaces. Apply the adhesive to both surfaces and glue together.

4 Ensure your piece is on a flat surface or is balanced so that it stays in position while the adhesive dries. It will be ready to handle after 8 hours but won't be fully hardened for 14 hours.

Resin

Resin is a liquid plastic that usually comes in two parts: the resin itself and a hardener (sometimes called an accelerator or catalyst). Follow the manufacturer's instructions to get the best results, but these tips will apply to most types of resin.

Working with resin

1 Make sure your work area is well ventilated, dry, and damp free. Cover the work surface in newspaper and ideally wear plastic gloves and goggles when mixing.

2 Get your mold ready before you start mixing. Molds must be clean and free from dust or grease. If need be, prop your mold upright using soft, oil-based modeling clay.

3 Have at least three disposable cups and mixing sticks handy for measuring and mixing your resin. Most types of resin stipulate 50% resin to 50% hardener. In this case, pour the right amount of resin for the project into the first cup. Mark a line on the outside where the resin rests. Then pour into the second cup.

4 Pour your hardener into the first cup up to the drawn line on the outside. Then add this to the measured resin in the second cup. Mix thoroughly with a disposable stick. The third cup is useful if you are adding color to your resin. If resin has different mixing ratios you can draw measurements onto the side of your first cup as a guide.

5 When thoroughly mixed, your resin will contain lots of air bubbles that will eventually disappear during the curing process. Pour your resin into the mold so that it slightly overfills—using its surface tension to keep it from spilling—and leave for at least 24 hours.

Using polymer clay

Polymer clay is very easy to work with and the projects in this
book require little in the way of special techniques.

Softening polymer clay

When you first open your packet of clay it will be quite solid. All
types of polymer clay require some softening (sometimes called
conditioning), to make them easier to mold and shape.

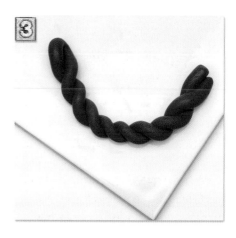

1 Take a chunk of clay from the pack
and begin to roll it between the palms
of your hands.

2 On your work surface, roll it into
a long sausage.

3 Bend and twist the sausage. Repeat
steps 2 and 3 until the clay feels soft
and pliable.

Tip *Every pack of polymer clay carries the manufacturer's instructions for baking.
This is generally a low heat, around 230°F (110°C), for about 30 minutes.*

Blending colors

Although you can buy a wide range of colors of polymer clay "off the shelf," it is very useful to know how to create your own customized shades. It is not difficult and will make your designs distinctive and unique. Once you have created that perfect color match you may want to re-create it again in the future. This method will avoid wasting clay and help you to keep a record of how a particular color was achieved.

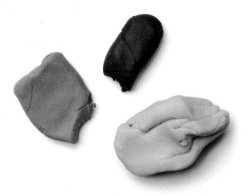

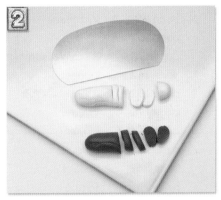

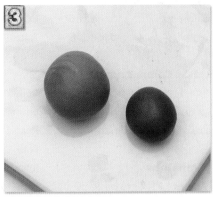

1 Roll two equal, finger-sized sausages of your "test" colors. Here, we are experimenting with red and white.

2 With a sharp blade, slice up both sausages into small, equal-size chunks. It doesn't matter how thin or thick the slices are, just that both colors are sliced evenly. Each slice is now a measured portion of clay.

3 Take one slice of each color, squash them together and knead thoroughly until the two colors are completely blended and no marbling is visible. From here, it is easy to experiment with different proportions to create new shades and colors, for example one slice of white and two of red. You may like to keep a note of the amounts of each color used each time. Once you find your perfect shade you can re-create it again and again by using those same proportions.

Acknowledgements

The publishers would like to thank the following people for their contributions to this book:

DESIGNS

Melanie Blaikie

Wildfire	page 22
Harmony	page 66
Cocktail	page 110
Romance	page 146
Effloresce	page 186
Luster	page 210

Louise Campagnone

Annie	page 34
Jacques	page 82
Tavi	page 126

Sarah Drew

Senorita	page 30
Faerie	page 74
Clarice	page 118
Flapper	page 150
Twinkle	page 218

Joan Gordon

Zoe	page 18
Pebbles	page 62
Mille	page 106
Jan	page 182
Chelsea	page 202
Leandri	page 214
Daisy	page 246

Sian Hamilton

Millie	page 14
Emily	page 26
Samba	page 42
Hannah	page 58
Coco	page 86
Alice	page 102
Trigger	page 130
Shari	page 142
Polly	page 162
Emma	page 178
Rose	page 206
Felix	page 226
Julia	page 242
Luna	page 258
Katie	page 266
Paddy	page 270
Jem	page 282
Kitty	page 294
Nala	page 310

Sophie Robertson

Beady	page 38
Cara	page 46
Night owl	page 78
Dreamcatcher	page 90
Decoupage	page 122
Amy	page 134
Pearly	page 158
Canary	page 166

Peacock	page 222
Roxy	page 230
Streamlined	page 254
Crystal	page 274
Songbird	page 286
Victoriana	page 298

Tansy Wilson

Honeybee	page 50
Chichi	page 54
Writing	page 70
La mer	page 94
Opo	page 98
Shapes	page 114
Tembo	page 138
Clusters	page 154
Knotty	page 170
Gecko	page 174
Buttons	page 190
Scoubidou	page 194
Skye	page 198
Cameo	page 234
Claudia	page 238
Florence	page 250
Audrey	page 262
Twists	page 278
Illusion	page 290
Spirals	page 302
Zippy	page 306

Index

To order a book, or to request
a catalogue, contact:

GMC Publications Ltd
Castle Place, 166 High Street,
Lewes, East Sussex,
BN7 1XU
United Kingdom
Tel: +44 (0)1273 488005
www.gmcbooks.com